# Weaving Tapestry
# in Rural Ireland

# Weaving Tapestry in Rural Ireland

## Taipéis Gael, Donegal

Meghan Nuttall Sayres

Photographs by Laurence Boland

Tapestries by Taipéis Gael

ATRIUM

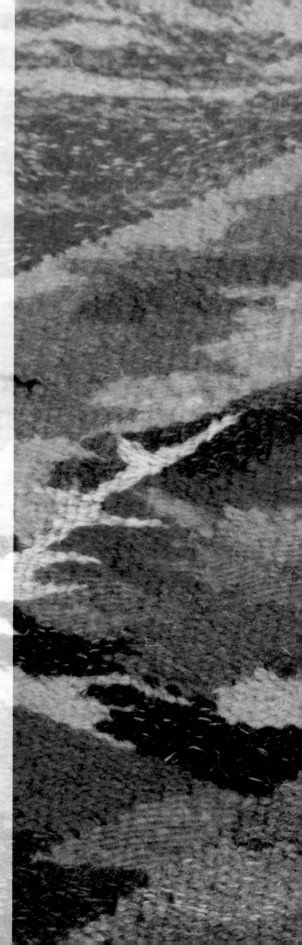

*Lorg an tSaoil,*
Traces of Life (detail),
Monica de Bath.

First published in 2006 by

ATRIUM

Youngline Industrial Estate

Pouladuff Road, Togher

Cork, Ireland

ATRIUM is an imprint of Cork University Press

Reprinted 2008

© Meghan Nuttall Sayres, 2006

British Library Cataloguing in Publication Data

A CIP catalogue record for this book is available from the British Library.

ISBN-10: 0–9535353–3-9

ISBN-13: 978–0-9535353–3-0

The author has asserted her moral rights in this work.

Designed at Bite Design, Cork

Printed by Graficas Cems, Navarra, Spain

This publication has received support from the Heritage Council under the 2006 Publications Grant Scheme.

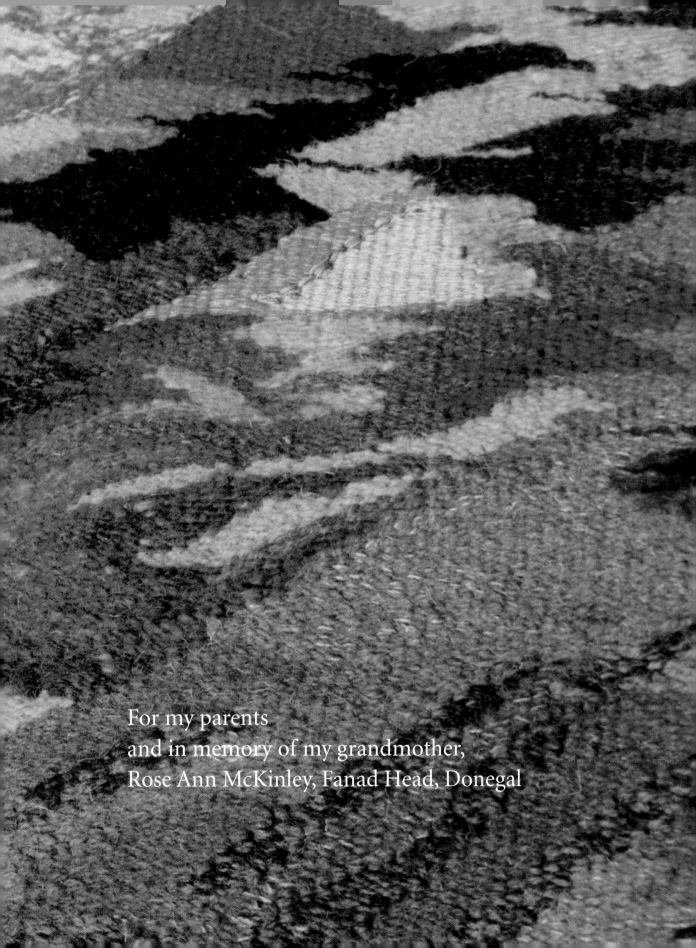

For my parents
and in memory of my grandmother,
Rose Ann McKinley, Fanad Head, Donegal

# Contents

St Columba's Church,
Church of Ireland,
Glencolmcille.

# Prologue

The summer I turned fifteen I lowered myself for the first time into an ancient souterrain, an underground ruin. It lay beneath the graves and high crosses at St Columba's church in the village of Glencolmcille, County Donegal. This church is the beginning and end of the local pilgrimage, *An Turas Cholmcille*, and was the meeting place for my sister Eileen, three friends and myself with Mr Jack Gildea, a friend of my parents from Philadelphia. Mr Gildea suggested we explore the souterrain, which he believed was part of an old monastic site. Local lore holds that it may have been used for refuge or storage in times of invasions and hardships – the Vikings, Normans, the Penal Laws among them.

Our bicycle ride to Glen from Ardara that day had been longer than expected: up one side of Glengesh Pass and down the other. I didn't know it then, but we had rolled by Jimmy Carr's house in the village of Meanacross, swerving around a few of his sheep in the road, and had stopped to fix a flat tyre in front of Dermot Cannon's home, eighteen years before he was born. Years later, I would come to know these men when a pleasant madness for wool, tapestry and my Irish heritage would take hold of me.

The six of us filed up the stone path to St Columba's. Scouting about, we searched among headstones for the souterrain's entrance. We brushed aside knee-high grass to find burial slabs with dates reaching back to early Christian times. We fingered rough-hewn, pagan pillar stones and climbed over walls to discover a crude altar. But we found no entrance.

Regrouping, we realized that none of us really knew what we were looking for. What exactly was a souterrain? Would its entrance be obvious? Would it even have a door? After all, hadn't it been used as a place to hide? My sister noticed a tuft of sod out of place underfoot and lifted it. Beneath lay a slate. Moving this stone, we found a hole large enough for an adult to slip through.

Jack Gildea lowered himself into the souterrain first. One by one, the rest of us followed. He struck matches so that we could see. From time to time, the flame lit up the crevices between the stones in the nearly airless, tomb-like room. I remember the smell of roots, the warmth of the others' bodies as we inched along in unison, and how the darkness pressed down. My diminished sight brought on a kind of ticklishness, a

Gravestone beside St
Columba's Church,
Church of Ireland,
Cashel.  Beneath
lies a souterrain, an
underground refuge
normally associated
with ringforts or
monastic settlements.
This one was
discovered in 1832 by
men who were digging
a grave.

This Pre-Christian
pillar stone beside
St Columba's Church
in Glencolmcille is
Station Two of *An
Turas Cholmcille,*
the local pilgrimage.
Taipéis Gael artists
draw from the designs
on these ancient rocks
for their own work.

*Exile*, Conal McIntyre, commercial and handspun yarn, 22"x45". This tapestry looks at the final chapter in St Colmcille's life (521-597 AD). St Colmcille founded monasteries and scholarly establishments in Ireland. After a battle with Dermot, the High King of Ireland, Colmcille left for Iona. With dark memories buried – represented in the tapestry by snakes crawling beneath the standing stone – he then blazed a trail that influenced the spread of Christianity in Scotland and throughout Western Europe.

'I wove this tapestry for an exhibition in Derry. In a sense, the standing stone is a symbol of death. The yellow and pink – or dawning sun – represents a moving toward new life. Colmcille brought a message of good news with him to Iona and beyond'.

Collection of Joseph M. Murphy, Country Bank, Scarsdale, New York

Photo: Joe Vericker/ Photo Bureau

Right: Pre-Christian dolmens, east-facing portal tombs bearing large capstones, are numerous in Glencolmcille and date back to approximately 2000 BC. In testament to those who came before, these archaeological sites provide inspiration for Taipéis Gael's work.

Far Right: *Siombaili Glencolmcille*, Margaret Cunningham, 18"x12", commercial yarns. This tapestry brings together archaeological symbols from the parish of Glencolmcille and is a gift presented to President Mary MacAleese by the parish.

'This tapestry links the region through stone. The design includes a dolmen from Malinmore; a holy well from Teelin; the Glencolmcille Angel (from a headstone); the bridge in Carrick and a stone wall built in Meenaneary by Oideas Gael students during a two-year Horizon course'.

Collection of President Mary MacAleese

Photo: Margaret Cunningham

girlish giddiness. With it came a keen awareness of something pulling me – drawing me in – like the earth above, below, and all around.

It is only now, some twenty-five years later, watching my children descend into this same subterranean passage, that I attach meaning to that magnetism I experienced back then. It left an impression as real as the cross-and-moon motif incised on the roof-lintel at the far end of the souterrain. Among those ruins, I felt as if the place itself held a speaking, watching presence. This pull would bring me back again and again to Glen's headlands, chiseled stones and sweeping strands, where I would eventually meet a group of tapestry weavers called Taipéis Gael – artists who have formed a cooperative with the help of mentors who taught them the old ways of spinning, weaving and dyeing wool. Having visited them in their kitchens and workrooms and listened to their stories, I can't help but wonder if they are keepers of something as ancient and long guarded as that souterrain and if something of the very land is woven into the work of Taipéis Gael.

Meghan Nuttall Sayres

# Introduction

# An Introduction to Taipéis Gael

This is a story about how in 1993 a group of tapestry weavers formed the cooperative Taipéis Gael (Gaelic Tapestries) with the help of older mentors in Glencolmcille, County Donegal. It is the tale of a ten-year journey, one that nurtured these young artists, encouraged them to exhibit their work, and brought them international praise. Tucked between mountainous headlands jutting into the North Atlantic on the most western tip of Ulster, these weavers preserve their heritage in contemporary tapestry. While weaving their legacy, they have created hundreds of pieces – a collection of woollen emissaries of highly imaginative motifs and hues. These works now grace the halls of museums, galleries, embassies, banks, pubs and private homes around the world. The work that has been created by Taipéis Gael has not only helped to bring recognition to the cooperative as a successful collaborative entity, but it has also helped to establish each of the artists in his or her own right. As Margaret Cunningham's tapestry *Ag Dul Siar In Am* (Time Warp) suggests, their work embodies a tension between the past and the infinite possibilities of the future. To hold one of their weavings is to voyage through other dimensions, not only forward and backward in time, but within and beyond the self. Indeed, to hold one of their weavings is to touch spirit.

PLACE AND PEOPLE

Glencolmcille lies about twenty miles west and slightly north of Killybegs. Its surrounding communities include Meenaneary, Carrick, Kilcar, Teelin, Malinmore and Malinbeg. These townlands are enlivened by poets, potters, painters, writers, musicians, knitters, quilters and sculptors, as well as the Taipéis Gael weavers.

Like others living in coastal towns of the Gaeltacht (the Irish-speaking regions of Ireland) Taipéis Gael weavers and their ancestors have experienced social, economic and educational deprivations that have forced many to leave the region for work. Historically, according to anthropologist and linguist Dr Eileen Moore Quinn, they have also received mixed messages about their identity, ranging from defamation to romantic idealism, including the suggestion that they most fully possess the characteristics considered to define Irishness. At the height of Ireland's cultural–nationalist revival in the late nineteenth and early twentieth centuries, the Irish-speaking populations served as *the* symbol for Irish identity, and the Gaeltacht received official definitive status.[1]

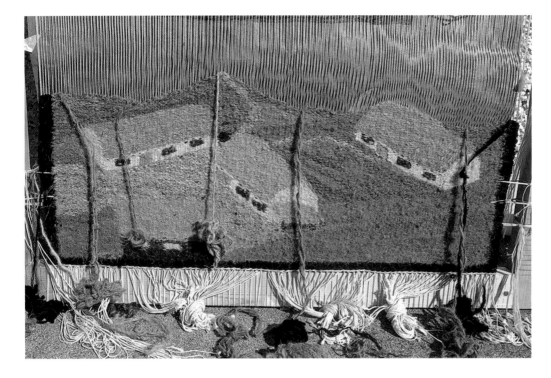

An on-loom detail of *An t-Athair Mac Daidhir – Aghaidh Glencolmcille* by Angela Byrne.

Collection of Angela Byrne

Photo: Margaret Cunningham

Writing under the name Kinnfaela, T. C. McGinley wrote about the people of the Gaeltacht (and more specifically those of Malinbeg, one of the townlands in which Taipéis Gael had rented a studio). About the people of Glencolmcille parish, he said, 'There is seldom any degree of relationship farther removed than second cousins. Accordingly, nearly all the family names here are O'Byrnes or MacGinleys'. He goes on to talk about the special pride the local people took in preserving the oral history of their ancestors. It seems this quality remains true today.[2]

In his 1978 book entitled *Bogmail* the native-born novelist Patrick McGinley describes the farmers and fishermen of this area through the eyes of a character named Potter, who says they are 'hardy, bony men who went out unthinkingly in all weathers. They were men who reminded him of bare uplands, grey rocks and forlorn roads in the mountains'.[3] These same people are discussed in Dr Quinn's dissertation by a manager at the Meenaneary fish factory who noted that the people were of three kinds: water, mountain and 'goodland'.

Of late, Glencolmcille has become a tourist destination containing both a folk village built in the 1960s under the direction of the late Father McDyer, as well as Oideas Gael, a more recent cultural college. Together they help attract students from around the world who come to learn Irish language, fiddle, archaeology, hill-walking among other things. In this centre Taipéis Gael wove its first tapestry.

*An Clachan*, Townland, is the folk village in Glencolmcille that features period houses spanning four centuries. It was one of the late Father McDyer's projects to generate work and tourism in the area.

Tourists needing accommodation spawned a healthy seasonal Bed and Breakfast trade in the area. Presently there are four restaurants, a café and a video-rental store. Other establishments in Glen include two wool shops, a tourist information centre, two convenience stores, one hotel, a hostel, a handful of pubs. There is also a primary school, a health centre, a post office, but no bank.

Although Glencolmcille sees steady business activity in late spring, summer and early autumn, there is little tourism in the winter. This contributes to the large proportion of residents receiving public assistance. In her dissertation, Quinn, who lived in Glencolmcille in 1995, noted 'a pattern of chain migration that operates from Glen to certain cities in the United States such as Boston and Chicago'.

WHISPERS FROM THE MARGINS

While some of Taipéis Gael's tapestries reflect the more nostalgic images, folklore and music of the Gaeltacht, the group defines itself beyond these parameters. They have travelled through Europe, the US, Africa and Australia exchanging ideas with artists of other cultures. They've hosted weavers from North and Central America as well as from Japan, and have entered into transnational collaborations and fora. After returning from a visit to the American Southwest, Margaret Cunningham wove a tapestry called *Famine Wall II* that illustrates this transcendence of place, while at

*An t-Athair Mac Daidhir—Aghaidh Glencolmcille*, Angela Byrne, 30"x 48," handspun and natural dyes. This tapestry is one of Angela's first, which she wove during the two-year training course with Taipéis Gael. She chose to weave this piece for her father in memory of Father James McDyer, who was a friend of her family. Angela's own father died before she finished this tapestry, giving the work another layer of meaning.

Father McDyer devoted thirty years of his life to the parish of Glencolmcille. He championed the building of a folk village called *An Clachan,* Townland, among other projects to bring tourists and revenue into the area. The folk village is made up of period cottages that span four centuries. One of the priest's poems hangs on the wall in a teahouse, recalling the spirit of his work ethic:

Let us not cease our sacrifices

And endeavors until the agony

Of emigration, the pinch of poverty

And the slur of indolence shall

Have been lifted from the brows of men.

—Rev. Fr. J. McDyer (1966)

Collection of Angela Byrne

Photo: Margaret Cunningham

The work of Taipéis Gael echoes a social responsibility, *comhair* in Irish, which seems inherent to their community. Like the fishermen, the sheep men often share boat rides to reach their flocks, which have been set to graze on a nearby island.

Left side of photo, stern to bow: Declan Byrne, James Curran, Liam Ellis, James McGinley.

Right side of photo, stern to bow: Taipéis Gael weavers Dermot Cannon, Conal McGinley (husband of Taipéis Gael weaver Máire McGinley), Patrick O'Gara and Mark Tubridy.

the same time honouring it. In her tapestry, she has incorporated a Native American fertility symbol called Kokapelli, along with the well-known Irish one, Sheela na Gig. The piece recalls the Cherokee Nation's contribution to the Irish during the Famine.

The work of Taipéis Gael echoes a social responsibility, *comhair* in Irish, which seems inherent in the community. Just as local fishermen share the same boat, or sheep men gather to shear a neighbour's flock, Taipéis Gael weavers wash, pick, and card fleece – wrestling local wool into art. In the end, everyone reaps their fair portion of what the harvest produces. 'Fraternity is inherent in a cooperative', says the founder of Taipéis Gael, Monica de Bath. 'This trust gives these weavers an advantage within the Irish arts community and internationally'. Monica believes that work created collectively can be more significant than work created individually. 'Often it is a dialogue from which powerful stories can be expressed'.

Unlike an independent artist, a group benefits from the ability to develop a body of work large enough to secure an exhibition more easily. Cooperatives may rise above the adage that when an artist is working, he or she is not selling and vice versa. In Taipéis Gael's partnership, someone stays home creating while another is abroad exhibiting.

Historically, isolation has worked against the rural Irish. Taipéis Gael tapestries reflect this and the hardships experienced by other minorities such as the Irish Travellers, whose voices are seldom heard. The weavers' images, in Monica's words, 'whisper from the margins'. They are silent statements giving texture to past and present issues: the Famine, emigration, family and fertility, women's issues, peace and reconciliation within Ireland, and intercultural collaborations on social justice.

PAST AND PRESENT

Taipéis Gael's tapestries did not bring a splash of colour to the eternal grey of the rock, or to the green of the hills in Glen, without help. Their success is won from the will of the young and from the skills of the old. With the good sense to look back, not only do the weavers build upon indigenous artistic abilities stemming from the Neolithic era, but they also draw from similar projects of other times.

In *Ireland's Traditional Crafts*, it is noted that sheep were introduced to Ireland 6,000 years ago and that there is archaeological evidence that spinning was practised at least 3,000 years ago.[4] The significance of spinning is demonstrated in early Brehon laws (600–800AD) which state that in the event of a divorce, a woman gets to keep her bride price, which would have consisted of spun yarn, spindles and related items.[5] In her recent book, *This is Donegal Tweed*, Judith Hoad suggests that the development of tweed weaving in Donegal depended on the developments in the linen industry

*Balla an Ghorta II, Famine Wall II*, detail of a larger work by Margaret Cunningham. Margaret has brought together Native American and Irish fertility symbols in this tapestry, which commemorates the contribution of the American Indians to the Irish during the Famine. It also illustrates the cooperative's transcendence of place, while at the same time honouring it by exploring aspects of other cultures in their work.

Collection of Joseph M. Murphy, Country Bank, Scarsdale, New York.

See p. 121 for full image.

Photo: Joe Vericker/ Photo Bureau

over the last 200 hundred years. This in turn evolved out of a long history in the area of flax production going back to the Bronze age.[6]

Today's climate for cooperatives in Ireland grew out of public policy started in the early nineteenth century. According to *Ireland: Industrial and Agricultural,* a book published in 1902 for the Department of Agriculture and Technical Instruction, many people believed that a doctrine of cooperative movements was required to stem the drain of emigration. The Northwest Agricultural Society was established in 1821 and the Agricultural Organization Society in 1894. One analyst reported that, although cooperative action was believed by some to be 'alien to the national temperament and habits', the farmers recognized the economic advantage that could be derived from 'co-operation in every branch of the business'. By 1902 the idea caught on in the poultry, flax-scutching, lace-making, embroidery and tweed-weaving industries.[7]

In *Ireland: Industrial and Agricultural* Lady Betty Balfour discusses the history of lace making. She says, 'The Cooperative Needlework Society which has been started at Dalkey has set an excellent example to girls everywhere in Ireland . . . Under this system the skilled and capable girl need not wait for an employer . . . Let them combine to procure the implements, materials, and technical training necessary for the production of a marketable article, and they have secured for themselves a livelihood'. [8]

Taipéis Gael received support from Údarás na Gaeltachta and was also funded in part by Horizon, a European Social Fund Initiative to combat social exclusion. Údarás promotes social, economic and cultural programmes in Irish-speaking communities with poor soil and harbours, and little industry or employment. Údarás' predecessor, Gaeltarra Éireann, was initially set up by the Irish parliament after Independence from the British in 1922. Before that the Congested Districts Board (CDB) served a similar geographic area. In the mid-1880s, the CDB aimed to assess and alleviate the bad conditions of the people in rural Ireland after the Famine. Through the Board's Donegal Industries Fund, classes were taught in Irish to help extend local skills, such as spinning, dyeing, tweed weaving, crochet and lace making. The Board then brought the handmade goods that were produced to the notice of buyers outside the country. 'These projects kept a pound in your pocket where there would otherwise be none', said Taipéis Gael mentor Mary McNelis, recalling the days in the 1950s and 1960s when she hand-knitted sweaters for Gaeltarra Éireann for four shillings and six pence each.

Another cooperative that still flourishes is the Irish Countrywomen's Association. This group, which was initiated by a woman whose father worked as an inspector for the CDB, set up the Country Shop in Dublin, a centre for handmade goods from all over Ireland. According to Hoad, many native craftsmen – weavers especially – would have lost all markets for their work if it were not for the Country Shop.

Other related organizations include the Dún Emer Guild, to which Lily Yeats (sister to Jack and William Butler) belonged. This guild, established in Dublin around 1900, designed and wove carpets and curtains, furniture coverings and tapestries. The Royal Dublin Society, founded in 1731, still holds an annual Exhibition of Arts and Industries at Ballsbridge. A century ago, lace-making would have held a prominent position there. In 1998 Taipéis Gael was a special guest of the RDS and was spotlighted on RTÉ television.

In his novel, *Bogmail*, Glencolmcille-born Patrick McGinley describes the farmers and fisherman of this area through the eyes of his character, Potter. He says they are 'hardy, bony men who went out unthinkingly in all weathers. They were men who reminded him of bare uplands, grey rocks and forlorn roads in the mountains'.

Locals say this is the late Daniel Paddy Mosey's horse from Carrick. Daniel walked these uplands with his sheep.

# Founder of Taipéis Gael, Monica de Bath

Monica de Bath was born in County Laois and grew up in Clonaslee, a small village at the foot of the Slieve Bloom mountains. She was taught by her mother in the local national school, who instilled in her a love of art and of Irish. She was only twelve when she was packed off to Anagry, her first taste of the Donegal Gaeltacht.

She has worked in community arts programmes linked with adult education and rural development in Ireland and Africa. At present, she is developing her own art practice and is also a consultant for the Irish Arts Council. In 1986 she travelled to Zimbabwe, where she taught fine art to ex-combatants and acquired accreditation and jobs for graduates of the Hamden Arts Institute in Harare. During her two years in Africa, she worked alongside the Zimbabwean weaver and tutor, Winnie Fernando, who introduced her to Cold Comfort, a cooperative that later provided part of Monica's motivation for establishing Taipéis Gael in 1993.

Monica continues to work toward group exhibitions with artists from Taipéis Gael. The cottage she keeps in Glencolmcille, 'her home away from home', allows her to take a hand in the group weaving shows, have an ear for the craic, and keep a nurturing eye on the community of weaver-artists she helped cultivate.

It was August in Glencolmcille, the week of the town's international fiddle festival. Traditional tunes seeped from the windows of homes, pubs and dew-drenched tents. On that day, Monica set a teapot and two china cups on a slate outside her cottage. She was preparing to tell me the details of how she came to form Taipéis Gael.

'When I was in Zimbabwe, the integration of music, textiles, painting, farming and building within the communities with which I worked made an impression on me', she said. 'I think subconsciously it made me think of the Irish ways of artistic expression. Traditional music came to mind, but those with a natural talent in the visual arts seemed to be silent. I knew Glencolmcille had a long history of tweed weaving and that wool is still abundant here. And I began to think how suited this place would be for a weaving cooperative. I believed if I dug, I'd find a way to unlock that talent'.

Looking toward the sea, she continued. 'When I was back in Glen I met an elderly man named Jimmy Carr, who had worked for a weaver when he was a young man. We had many a long talk about weaving and about the possibility of pulling together

Monica de Bath,
Taipéis Gael founder,
holding dyer's
chamomile beside the
cottage she keeps in
Glencolmcille.

a project in Glen. From Jimmy I got a sense of the urgency around the need to save the indigenous skills of natural dyeing, spinning and weaving from ending up in the grave with the old people, and the need to inspire the young to take pride in their rich cultural heritage.

'They have a unique way of seeing life here, which is informed by rugged mountains, coastal life and an ancient heritage that is visually obvious in the archaeology of Glen. If it hadn't been for Jimmy – he had such an enthusiasm about the idea – I may never have taken the notion of a weaving cooperative to Liam Ó Cuinneagáin, the administrator of Oideas Gael, the local cultural college. I had always dreamed of working here in Glencolmcille. This project made the otherwise unlikely opportunity a possibility'.

Since Oideas Gael was already well established, Monica thought that the college might lend its business expertise to an infant cooperative. She thought that since Glen receives a fair amount of tourists each summer, visitors might provide a local market for tapestries.

'I explored grants for the arts. When I finally found one that might apply to this project, its deadline was only three days away. Liam and I knew the chances of receiving aid would be stronger if the project were written up under the auspices of Oideas Gael, an established not-for-profit business'.

'When I received the application forms from Horizon EU Programme, there was no time to find a typewriter. I handwrote the application sitting at my kitchen table and sent it in. I recall Liam cringed when I told him I'd done this, but there simply wasn't time. Within a week or two I heard from the development fund. Horizon said they liked the project and if we could please fill out another typed application, they would formally consider us'.

Monica glanced at three children running to the football pitch beyond the dunes past the fuchsia that was in full bloom. 'When the initial funding came through, I quit my teaching job in Monaghan. Jimmy Carr helped me to advertise and recruit weavers for the cooperative. He knows just about everyone in Glen and this part of Donegal, particularly the people of his own generation who would have had a hand in weaving in the forties and fifties, when Glen was producing tweed for local and export markets.

'We drove around for two days in my car, putting little notices up in shops, at bingo, places where people gather. Six people responded. So we invited them to Oideas Gael, where Liam had offered us rent-free space for the first two years. We served tea. I showed the participants a bit about design and demonstrated tapestry weaving on a loom I'd made from a large picture frame.

'But it was only three of the six that day who were truly suitable for the project. So

*An t-Imirce*, Emigration, Máire McGinley, 29"x 48," handspun and natural dyes. A group of people leaving the *uiag* dock at Malinbeg for a sailing vessel or 'coffin ship' to take them to America. Máire has woven her present-day neighbours in the foreground of this piece.

This tapestry was Máire's first. It sold only weeks after being cut from the loom at the Milwaukee Irish Festival – the first sale for the new cooperative. Horizon, an EU development organization, chose this piece for promotional materials on their books, posters and postcards. The tapestry appeared on national television after Taipéis Gael's first exhibition at the Galway Arts Centre.

'This took several months to weave. When I first started out, the others teased me that my people's legs looked like sausages. I thought, "Oh, my God!" but I kept on going…I think it was my best tapestry in terms of story. It all came from myself, really. It wasn't like copying a design from a standing stone and filling it in. Because of the theme – emigration – it had to be subdued in colour. It's a sad scene and the natural dyes fit'.

Collection of Mary June Hanrahan

Photo: Horizon

we continued to knock on doors for another two to three weeks and decided to hold interviews and a second workshop at our studio. Initially, people had the tweed weaving in mind. It was hard for them to think about weaving as anything but tweed. So we thought we should explore fabric weaving in case some of the weavers would prefer the traditional weaving to tapestry. We asked Con O'Gara, a local weaver who makes rugs and wall hangings on a traditional Donegal loom, to come and demonstrate tweed weaving'. However, Taipéis Gael didn't own a traditional floor loom, and none was to be found in the village. 'Con O'Gara restores and sells them. He'd been so efficient at this, we had to go to Innishowen to buy one of Glen's own back!'

The weavers carried the heavy loom parts (reed, heddles, fly-shuttle and two 3-metre-wide beams on which the warp, and eventually the fabric, is rolled as it is woven) piece by piece, up to their second-floor studio and assembled it. This process took nearly a week to set up, thread and all.

'But after Con's workshop, everyone seemed a bit leery of working with such a loom. They wanted to start right in with the tapestry. They took to its simplicity, I think'.

Tapestry looms can be as rudimentary as a picture frame – the kind Taipéis Gael weaves on. Warp is threaded around nails or grooves along the top and bottom of the frame. Tapestry allows a certain freedom of design. Beginners can form shapes, such as curved lines, more readily in tapestry than on a traditional loom, where images can only emerge line by line and appear more geometrical.

Topping up my tea, Monica said, 'Jimmy and Mary Kate O'Gara taught the cooperative carding and spinning. Mary Kate would be one of the few left in Glen who had this skill. She came down to the studio for the Open Days, and for others after that. She would spin and spin and spin, all the while chatting and teaching. Mary Kate still talks about her younger years when women spun in each other's houses to pass the time. "There was no joy in it at all," she'd say. "The romance wasn't there. Not when you spun for your own sustenance"'.

Eventually, the interviews and workshops produced the six potential weavers needed to form Taipéis Gael: Margaret Cunningham, a local singer and musician in her twenties from Carrick; Dermot Cannon, a teenage neighbour of Jimmy Carr's whose family's sheep would later supply wool for the cooperative, and twenty-two-year-old Conal Gillespie whose flock did the same. There were also Sandra Mockler and Angela Byrne, both in their early twenties. The sixth was Máire McGinley, a mother of three from Malinmore. Five years later, they would be joined by Conal McIntyre, born in Malinbeg, who had just returned from a year in Australia, where he had taken up stone sculpture. (Sandra eventually left to study cookery in Letterkenny, and returned to run the restaurant housed in Oideas Gael with her sisters. Angela emigrated to London after two years and Conal later left the sheepfolds and clamour of the pubs where he pulled pints with his brothers for carpentry work in Chicago.)

Monica recalled the day Máire McGinley attended the recruiting workshops. 'Máire had come to the workshops with her sixteen-year-old, thinking perhaps this project might suit her daughter. But by the end of the day, her daughter wasn't interested – she was mad in love with the idea of moving to Belfast. So Máire said, "I think I'll try it myself". As it turned out, Máire's first tapestry, *Emigration,* was selected by Horizon for promotional literature and posters'.

*Emigration* also appeared on national television and in *The Irish Times* after Taipéis Gael's first exhibition at the Galway Arts Centre. A man in Milwaukee read the article and invited the weavers to the Milwaukee Arts Festival that year, where *Emigration* was sold – the first sale for the fledgling cooperative. The same tapestry caught the eye of two New York art collectors, one for whom Máire wove a similar piece, and another who commissioned several Famine pieces, one from each weaver. According to Monica, 'These initial sales gave the weavers motivation to keep with the project as well as tapestry, rather than any other form of weaving'.

For the first two years, Taipéis Gael weavers participated in a National Certificate course in art and design through a regional vocational education institute, wherein they completed a portfolio and an exam. Different aspects of the course were taught by Monica de Bath, along with colleagues in Ireland and artists from other countries. The weavers participated in textile workshops in Ireland and Denmark. They explored rug weaving with Sandra Mockler's uncle, Matt Mockler. Once again, they hauled out the traditional loom, which Matt kept stored for them in his shed. He spent almost a year working with Taipéis Gael until each weaver had completed a rug.

Taipéis Gael invited weavers to come from Guatemala to teach weaving techniques. 'They brought us a new appreciation for colour. Their brightly dyed clothing made a strong contrast to the dark colours of the Glen landscape'. The Guatemalan weavers, whose work often includes stories of their people, brought with them a perspective about textiles as an expressive art, rather than craft. 'While these women visited with us', Monica said, 'forty of their people, including poets, teachers, writers, health workers and weavers, were killed as they tried to reclaim their village. I'm sure their story reinforced for us the importance of our work, and of art in general, as a potentially powerful voice in times of peace and conflict'.

In those first two years, the weavers also experimented with natural dyes. 'Jimmy Carr was a tremendous help in this respect. He seemed to pull the recipes right out of himself for the heather, the bracken and the lichens'.

The group also worked with professional textile artists. Una Ní Sé, from the Údarás na Gaeltachta Arts and Crafts Centre in Dingle, taught felt-making and chemical dyeing. Theresa McKenna, of the National College of Art and Design, helped with the composition of one of their first large tapestries, 5 x 3 metres, titled *Lorg an tSaoil* (Traces of Life).

'We made the loom for this piece out of scaffolding large enough for all of us to weave on together'. *Lorg an tSaoil* is an abstract mapping of man and animals around a court cairn, a prehistoric burial site characteristic of the archaeological structures found around Glencolmcille. It features mainly landscape. The river running through it contains symbols of pagan and Christian markings found on the pillar stones in Glen, fossilized fish bones, sheep hooves and Máire's daughter's handprint, which represents the present. It was bought for the art collection of the Donegal County Council and hangs in the county library.

Little by little, the weavers' tapestries sold. Four became covers for poetry collections. Exhibition reviews and essays about their cooperative made their way into a handful of newspapers and journals in Ireland, Europe, Japan and the United States.

Monica continued, 'These articles brought students and commissions mostly from America and at the same time boosted the weavers' belief in themselves'. Breaking into a smile, she said, 'Even Hollywood gave us a ring one day. Someone there had read an article about us in *Ireland of the Welcomes* magazine. Their writers had been working

on a script about an Irish potter and thought maybe they should make him a tapestry weaver instead! I think the fellow who phoned was a bit surprised when we told him tapestry isn't an indigenous Irish craft. They must have dropped the idea. We never heard from them again'.

Despite the fact that news of Taipéis Gael had travelled to Hollywood, Monica said, 'But the reality is we're quite isolated up here. It's hard even making a run to the bank, thirty kilometres to Killybegs. What's exciting of late is that the Arts Council of Ireland has entered into a partnership with Údarás na Gaeltachta to actively support the development of the arts in the Gaeltacht. Such an alliance will help Taipéis Gael and other potential artists in Gaeltacht areas like Glencolmcille'.

Monica looked at her watch. It was time for her fiddle lesson. Working, weaving, all-night fiddle sessions – is it any wonder that her seemingly endless energy inspires a group of weavers to pool their talent and create images from wool that will live for generations?

Retired tweed weaver and local community leader Jimmy Carr with his motorbike outside Oideas Gael cultural college, home of Taipéis Gael's first studio.

# Mentors

Several people in Glencolmcille had a hand in mentoring the weavers at Taipéis Gael. Those I've included in this section have helped in different ways. Jimmy Carr, a store of cultural knowledge, community leader and former tweed weaver; Con O'Gara, a tweed and rug weaver and loom restorer; Mary McNelis, a local knitter and entrepreneur whose knitting factory helped to stem emigration; Rose Hegarty, a knitter and former natural dyer whose openness to the creative muse offered inspiration and affirmation to aspiring tapestry artists.

Most of these mentors are one or two generations older than Taipéis Gael. Some keep a hand in the craft of their art daily. All of them have kept the skills alive in memory, and have voluntarily and enthusiastically passed them on to Taipéis Gael.

Con O'Gara's business sign for his hand-woven rugs catches the breeze, as well as the eyes of people passing by.

# Mary McNelis

I first met Mary McNelis in 1994. Two or three miles from Glencolmcille, in the townland of Malinmore, she sat behind a small counter inside her modest retail store, the Rossan Sweater Factory. Beside floor-to-ceiling shelves stocked with machine-knit Aran garments, she knitted a sweater. 'I always like to keep my hands busy', she said.

I'd often dreamed of spending a month or more in Ireland to hone my handwork. So when I asked Mary then if she would someday teach me to knit, she told me that not long before, two German women had come into her shop for sweaters and had asked her the same thing. 'They rented a cottage and I taught them', she said.

Four years later, I found myself seated next to an electric heater inside Mary's newly enlarged store. Through the window, the colour of the bracken was vivid orange in the grey November light. The bald hill opposite her store was speckled with purple heather still in bloom. She showed me the correct way to knit an Aran diamond pattern. My attempts had produced weak, leftward-slanting stitches. Mary easily noticed my mistakes.

We talked about many things her recent trip to Germany, where she visited longtime customers, how her business began, and how it was for a mother of four to start her own enterprise in the Gaeltacht in the late 1960s and early 1970s.

'No one paid me no mind, a woman starting a business. I was a young mother then. What I really wanted to do was to get out of my kitchen!

'The story is, actually, that I worked on a domestic machine at home in the kitchen when the children were small. But as the children grew bigger, the kitchen got smaller and it was beginning to be a problem. And you know, in the old houses, the sitting room was also the kitchen. People used to come all the time to the door, inquiring if this was the place to go for sweaters, and there we'd be in the middle of dinner or cleaning up. So I looked into the possibility of receiving a grant to build a small building, just enough for a knitting machine and maybe a bit of shelving to display garments. Gaeltarra Éireann, now known as Údarás na Gaeltachta, a government-sponsored, rural development agency, provided three-quarters of the cost.

'I knitted through the winter and through the spring. In the beginning of July, I put a sign up at the top of the road', she said, waving a hand in the direction of the Glen Hotel. 'A very simple one: "Knitwear For Sale". It was mainly children's jackets. By the end of the season, I had everything sold.

'The next winter, I did the same. I took down my sign and worked through to spring. My oldest boy was thirteen and going to vocational school in Carrick. He used to wear

the garments and parents began to come to him and say, "Could your mother do me one of those?" The result was, of course, that he got interested in the knitting and less interested in the schooling, and he began to take the orders himself.' She laughed. 'He'd come home from school and fling the bag to the other end of the house. He would get on to the machine and chances are he'd have the garment back to them the next day!

'Not long after that, Father McDyer, the parish priest in Glencolmcille, talked him into dropping out of school and working in the Glen sweater factory, where he became very bored. He thought about doing construction work in England instead. But I said to him, "Look at your hands, they've never seen work like that. You won't survive". I asked him if an industrial machine would make him happy.

'So we bought the industrial machine and my son went to a twelve-week production course in Letterkenny. He met and teamed up with a Trinity graduate. They ran our business together for some time, then eventually split. His partner opened a factory in Kilcar. 'Today, both my sons and two of my three daughters work for Rossan. We have twenty employees. I never dreamed it would come to all of this!' She smiled as she looked about.

'I gave up the machine knitting as soon as my children took over the business, and I went back to my handknitting. I never really liked the machine.

Entrepreneur Mary McNelis in the showroom of the Russan Sweater Factory in Malinmore. She began her knitwear business from her kitchen in the late 1960s. It grew to include two buildings – a factory and store. Thirty years later, her business sense and artistic flair are an inspiration to Taipéis Gael.

'My girls get after me now when I carry my knitting over here everyday. And maybe I don't do ten stitches through a day, but I still have to have it there just in case'.

Mary remembered knitting in school at age seven. She sold her first sweater when she was a teenager to Gaeltarra Éireann, which ran the tweed-weaving enterprise in Glencolmcille. The tweed project was called the Mart.

'Eventually, the Mart closed, but Gaeltarra Éireann kept their main factory out in Kilcar. Gaeltarra used to come with a lorry-load of yarn every week. And all the weavers and knitters would go collect their bags of yarn for weaving or knitting jumpers in their own homes.

'You had to stand for two hours in a queue to get yarn. It was always on a Thursday you went. And the garment that you left on the previous Thursday was the one you'd get paid for. In the meantime the jumpers were sent to Galway, where they were checked for flaws. If there was the slightest fault, instead of your money coming back, your garment came back. You had to correct whatever was wrong before you were paid'.

A customer drove into Mary's carpark. Four women entered her store and browsed among the sweaters. Outside the window, shades of orange and purple streaked the sky where the sun plunged into the Atlantic.

Mary chatted with the women, bagged up the sweaters they bought, and sent them off with a blessing for their journey. Sitting next to me again at the sewing table, she said, 'Last summer was a bad tourist season, but we couldn't complain now. It's funny – on a wet day you get people coming into a place like this whereas normally, if it's a good day, they're away at the beaches or walking'. She pulled the electric heater closer, and continued, 'We were talking about knitting for Gaeltarra Éireann – I started off making children's Fair Isle sweaters with yarn that was so fine. I don't know where they were getting the yarn, it was so very fine. I remember the first two jumpers I made were size 24, which would be for a two- or a three-year-old, and what I got – it was the old money in them days – was four shillings and six pence each! Not even a pound. But you know, you could go to a dance for two shillings in those days.

'We all knitted Fair Isles for Gaeltarra Éireann for a few years until the Aran sweaters became fashionable. I think they became popular with the Clancys. You remember the Clancy Brothers? They went to America wearing the Aran sweaters.

'I earned twenty-one shillings in old money for an Aran sweater. And it took most of a week to knit it'.

I asked for clarification. 'Is that about four euro?' I asked, roughly four dollars.

Mary nodded, her expression showed a trace of exasperation.

'In the houses where there were two or three knitters, they were doing great, or so they thought. There was no money in those days, but people didn't need money the way they need it now, you know.

'They had turf, vegetables, their own milk, their own eggs. There was no rent to pay, they usually owned their own houses. There was no electricity, so they didn't have the kind of expenses they have now. People didn't need money except to buy maybe tea and sugar.

'Electricity didn't come until the fifties. But up on the mountain, where Jimmy Carr lives, it came even later. Electricity made all the difference, of course. There were no televisions before then. There were no phones either. If you wanted to send a message abroad it'd have to be a telegram from the post office. Once the electricity came, everything followed'. Mary paused and glanced at the ceiling. 'Then people felt they had to have everything. But you know, when you think back now, it was terrible wasn't it? Yet still people seemed to be happy. You have to ask yourself, do we need it all? Because we were happy before we ever got it'.

Mary explained that the sweater factory didn't just add to the family income and help get her out of the kitchen, but it also helped fight something much larger.

'My business was for money, of course, but all people ever talked about was emigration, just waiting for families to grow up and emigrate. I thought what a terrible way to live, you know, to bring up a family – big families at the time, maybe nine and ten in a house

– and all they ever thought about', she said, raising her hand toddler-height from the floor, 'from when they were so high, was about leaving. I always thought that was sad. If they go from choice, that's fine. But if they go from necessity, that's what is sad about it'. She gazed out of the window, then considered my knitting. 'You're doing grand, just grand'. I thought of how Taipéis Gael – having brought recognition and employment to this corner of south-west Donegal – has had the same effect as Mary's business and sees the stemming of emigration as a primary aspect of its mission. While the cooperative lost Angela Byrne to England and Conal Gillespie to Chicago, it has also helped four men and women to stay.

'Now I have one daughter who went to England and decided to stay there. England was the place for her. And that's fine. She went for choice and she never looked back. But when you go to England and Irish people living there say, "Would we not give anything to be able to live back home". I think that's what's sad'. Mary adjusted her glasses on her face and folded her hands on the table in front of her. 'Of course times have changed and there's a better life in Ireland than ever before – but there's not a lot of work for them to return to here in Glen. Many of the homes that were abandoned years ago are in ruin now. But, because of our factory, four out of five of my children were able to stay'.

Looking about Mary's store, it's obvious that business is thriving. Tables are piled with sweaters in several styles: cardigan and pullover crew necks and roll necks, short-waisted and long; racks are filled with tweed waistcoats, with woven handbags dangling off the sides; baskets are bursting with hats, gloves, and scarves.

'When we went into business, we went into it in a big way. From the mid-1970s, we catered to the tourist trade and later the export markets. We sold our sweaters in America, Germany, France and Sweden. Before we knew it, we had to enlarge our factory space and then we needed a larger show room. Údarás na Gaeltachta had built a factory down the road which was available just about the time we needed one. So we rented that, moved our knitting machines into it, and left the original building for a showroom'.

Mary's sons prefer the Údarás factory to their old one. Her daughters like having heavy equipment in a separate building, as this helps with the grandchildren who come to the shop with their mothers while they work.

Mary explained that, after the sweater machines were moved to the new factory, her daughters proposed to set up the newly remodelled showroom to work with tweeds.

Mary handed me a handbag and a blanket, which one of her daughters had sewn from swatches of handloomed tweed. We spread it between us.

'The sweaters were just a job for my girls, but the knitwear was the thing and they went along with it. Yet they always had this idea at the back of their minds about tweed – maybe mix and match and do this thing and that thing with tweed but there was never time to explore it. They were always up to their eyes with the knitting.

'We're having a designer come next week. She'll spend a few days down at the sweater factory, then a few days here working up new products with tweed. We hope to make tweed jackets. I think the handwoven tweed is beautiful'.

'Will you set up an old fly-shuttle loom here?' I asked.

'Ah, we'll use a traditional loom, of course', she said, gathering up the blanket and folding it. 'I remember the time when practically every house had a weaver'. Placing the tweed blanket back on the shelf and sitting down again, she continued, 'Just the same, I'll always have handknits for sale in my store. Only my own work. I'll tell you what I think the quality of the handknitting, it's gone down. For the simple reason that very few young people now do handknitting. The young people have no interest. They tell you their mothers have done it, their grandmothers have done it. It was slave labour. They were never paid. Now they're at school and they're twenty years old. They're educated for something that will give them better pay. It'll be gone in another ten years. There will be no handknitters left'.

'How do you feel about that?' I asked, 'The craft slipping away'.

'I can't see being the one to inspire the young to knit. There's no living to be made in it. You know, so many people have asked me over the years how long it takes to knit an Aran sweater and I could never tell them because I'd pick it up now and again and put it down and so on until the thing was finished. But I finally timed myself knitting a sweater. Fifty-eight hours. That's after fifty years' experience. And today handknitters are paid £22–23 at most by agents for export to America.

'So that shows you. It's finished, definitely. But maybe not in my time. I'll still do it because I love it!'

I asked Mary to see some of her work and she showed me the sweater she had just finished: a traditional style pullover with a crew neck. It is a heathery blue-green, much the colour the bracken on the bald hill opposite her store will look come spring.

Pointing to her sweater's patterns, she named them. 'That's the blackberry stitch. Here's just a cable. That would be half a diamond – well, that's just my own idea. I don't like doing them all the same. I like changing them slightly'.

Mary reached for my knitting, and picked up the stitch I had just dropped.

'I'm worried I'll forget all the knitting wisdom you've passed on to me over the years', I said.

'Just keep it in front of you', she said. 'It'll all come back to you'.

# Con O'Gara

It was black in the shed, except for the cone of light coming from a lone bulb. Beneath it, Con O'Gara sat at his loom. He pulled the weft beater and the shuttle flew side to side with a loud *clock* – the smack of metal against wood, splitting the darkness.

'Oh, I've been weaving 500 years', he joked. 'Made the loom myself. Would you like one? I'll have all the parts you need restored and shipped to your door for a thousand pounds. Sent one to Perth not long ago'.

Con smoothed his hands across blue and green threads inching up and across the warp, then adjusted the winter cap he wore above his ears to keep the crown of his head warm. Dust hung on the beam and heddles. Wool lint collected at his feet.

'Some people think my shed's a mess, but I've got to be able to see the colours. I can't choose a yarn when the spools are neatly placed on a shelf. They've got to be spread about me where I can see 'em and reach 'em'.

Moving to a stool beside his loom, he stepped on soft bits of yarn, unravelled sweater sleeves, and piles of throw rugs. Here he's attached an old bicycle wheel rim, its spokes intact. 'This is my bobbin winder', Con said, slipping a bobbin onto a steel spindle, a needle-like rod that is embedded in the side of his loom. He wrapped thread from a bolt yarn on the floor around the bobbin and gave the wheel a spin, setting spindle and bobbin into motion. Yarn from the bolt wound rapidly about the bobbin, which he later inserted into his shuttle. I mentioned the bicycle wheel on a loom in Malinmore in the Weaver's Bar. 'Aye, I restore the old looms as I can. Education institutions like to buy them.

'I find 'em in barns. But many have rotted in Glen. People stuck pieces of looms in the ground for gate posts, or they put them out in the shed and the roof would cave in, or the looms got eaten by wood worm.

'I usually find the frames and the sleas and the heddles. The other parts I have to make, like the foot treadles.

'Would you like to buy a rug?' He pointed to three shelves on either side of his workspace filled with weavings. Hundreds of them. 'I'm told President Mary McAleese chose one of these natural mohair rugs. The tourist information shop in Glen always keeps a few in stock'. His grin told me perhaps he's pulling my leg. 'They're hard to sell. You see the first thing people will buy is drink. The next thing they'll buy is food. And

Con O'Gara at work
inside his weaving
shed beside the Murlin
River. Con taught
Taipéis Gael artists the
basics of weaving on
the traditional Donegal
loom, the kind he
enjoyed restoring.

if they any money left, they might buy a rug. Very hard to sell. You wouldn't be making a living at it.

'Would you like to buy a spinning wheel?' he asked, pointing to the ceiling where antique wheels and flyers hang from the rafters. 'I sold antiques in England where I worked after the war'.

Con closed the wooden door to his concrete weaving shed. Water from the Murlin River murmured beyond us – a stream filled with stars. Leaves rustled. In daylight, Con enjoys a view of the river and a cluster of walnut trees from a window in his studio.

He led the way into his whitewashed house through the front door, stoked the peat fire in the living room, and pulled up two chairs.

'Used to be a loom in every house in Glen. There were sixty weaving here at one time, up until the 1970s. Power looms took over. And you couldn't compete with the power loom. Only thing you can make now is something the power loom can't make and that's rugs. Couldn't make tweed now and compete. Tweed-weaving is a dying trade. Young people wouldn't be doing it'.

He explained that tweed-weaving began in Glen around 1920 or 1930. Gaeltarra Éireann sponsored it for about forty years. Most weavers worked at home, although some wove at a factory in Kilcar, a village about nine miles away.

'We used to make army shirts. It was the first part of tweed weaving, really. They were made of pure wool. The weave was very fine: twenty-seven shots to the inch, twenty-seven picks. You worked long hours. You had your own time, you had no contract. The weaver made £1.50 for ninety yards. Imagine. About £1.50 a week. If you worked very hard you might make £2. That's how everybody started weaving, more or less. No, it was good in its day.

'When the war was over, they started making Donegal tweed. Then it got slack, then it came on again for a while and they built the factory here in Glen in the sixties. It was called the Mart. There were about twenty-four or twenty-five people weaving in it, I think. It was good in its day, oh yeah, it was good. But then they brought in the double-width looms. Mine's a single-width loom. All scrapped in the end'.

He got up to throw another sod of peat onto the fire.

'Cup of tea?'

As he walked to his kitchen, I asked him who'd have come all this way to buy fabric. 'Magee's, in Donegal town. But they sold to markets in London and New York, as well. We were only a drop in the ocean, really.

'You take sugar, do you?' he said, coming back into the room, where we sat. 'Paddy Boyle still weaves at home for Magee's. They're the big manufacturers. They've a few handweavers out in the country, even now. But really what's happening is Magee's sell sports jackets to Americans. The people who are buying them think they're buying handwoven tweed. But most of it is power loom woven. They keep a few hand weavers on so they can keep the name.

'You see, the difference between hand-loomed and power-loomed tweed is in the selvage. The power loom doesn't turn over. The power loom takes the thread over and cuts it. Then, it takes another one over. This leaves a fringe on both sides of the fabric. The handloom takes the thread across and turns it over and turns it back, leaving a finished edge. Very few know that'.

Con's point is reiterated by Judith Hoad, a Donegal woman who has written extensively about the history of tweed weaving in the region. Hoad says it is the romance of the hand-production – the sheep on the hills, the handspinners in cottage doors and the handloom weavers at work in thatched sheds – that is part of the appeal for customers who may, at the end of the day, buy a piece of power-loomed cloth without realizing it.[1]

Since the mid-1950s, most textile designers, particularly in America, buy 58-inch fabric made on power looms. Single-width looms make 28-inch fabric and take four times longer to produce a web. In 1957, the Donegal Handwoven Tweed Association, a cooperative effort between Magee's, Molloy's, McNutt's and Gaeltarra Éireann, successfully lobbied the American Congress to keep import tariffs for 28-inch fabric at

5 per cent when 58-inch fabrics faced quotas and 20 per cent taxes. The romantic image of the poor Donegal tweed weaver helped the Association to convince the American lawmakers. These rates apply today and make it economically feasible for Donegal companies to keep producing hand-loomed tweed.

However, the fly-shuttle looms were not completely scrapped in the end.

Con pushed himself back into his chair. 'The art of spinning and carding is a thing of the past. The young girls wouldn't know how to do it. Handknitting is a thing of the past, too. At one time, during the Big War, they had a great industry going here. They had the homespun. And you know what they started doing? They'd spin 80 yards. Then they'd scour it themselves, clean it, put it in boiling water. And they would pull 20 extra yards, stretch it so that they'd finish up with 100 yards. They would roll it on a roller and dry it. But if you went out and had a jumper on and you got wet, the sleeves would take up to your elbows and go back to its original shape! And it spoiled the business then. It spoiled it, aye. They brought it on themselves.

'So many machines now. So many machines knitting. Electric machines. And there's only one man walking up and down the aisle. Marvellous, eh? It's not labour intensive anymore. 'But the handknits, a good one is great. Great. If you get the good wool and good knitter, a handknit sweater is a mighty job. But the poor woman who knits it only gets about £20 and they finish up selling it at Magee's for £120. It's the middle man that spoils it. I know these shops have to make a profit…' His voice trailed off, avoiding a discussion about the full complexity and scope of the modern economy.

Some thirty years before Con was born, weaving took precedence over knitting as the principal craft in Glencolmcille. The Donegal Industrial Fund, which succeeded the Congested Districts Board, distributed hundreds of spinning wheels to Donegal, many intended for flax production. 203 wheels were distributed in Glencolmcille by 1891–2. The yarn spun on these wheels supplied seventeen weavers who wove 121 thirty-to-sixty yard webs in six months. The town of Malinbeg claimed for thirty wheels and one weaver that year. It seems the Congested Districts Board provided quality control, and private agencies oversaw marketing.

Con spoke of antique dealing and his work for the Irish Export Board in England after World War II. 'I used to give weaving exhibitions there, in Southampton and Coventry. Even had one of my old looms over there with me', he said, and smiled.

He got up to show me a textbook on spinning wheels. His interest in the history of weaving and the textile trade, his restorative work on looms, and the enjoyment he seems to get from the process of the craft itself, is apparent. I suspect it's for these reasons that he became involved with Taipéis Gael, because of his commitment to pass on what he knows of weaving, as an act of preservation.

Con said, 'Taipéis Gael, you think they'll keep going? I could not do what they're doing – tapestry. It's too slow a process for my liking. I taught them for a while. I had a loom there once. I spent a few weeks with them. Showed them how to do it, the weaving. That's what they started off on.

'Their tapestries are great when they're finished, but it's so time consuming, isn't it? Too labour intensive. And yarn can be very dear these days. I recycle the stuff myself, you know.

'I buy my yarns from the knitting factory store. The yarn left on the spools that they can't use. Not enough of any one colour. I buy that from them. Mix it all up. Or buy the pullovers that have a fault in them, you know? That they can't sell, wouldn't sell. I buy them. Rip them back. Recycle them'.

'Is anything else recycled in Glen?' I asked.

He replied, 'The only thing recycled in Glen is wool'.

But what comes to my mind is the recycled land in this region of Ireland, how it has passed from one people to the next, from one generation to the next. Pre-Christian pillar stones here evolved to become part of Christian traditions. One such stone – incised with circles, crosses and lines – stands a few paces from Con's house. It is Station Fourteen of *An Turas Cholmcille,* the local pilgrimage. How the houses have changed over time, from thatch to slate, from one storey to two, and even to two-and-a-half or as one local calls this kind of structure, 'a house half-high, half-low'. And most resourcefully, how the ruins of old sheds, walls, famine houses and monasteries have become sheepfolds. To say nothing of Con himself, recycling looms.

And so I asked, 'Would you agree Taipéis Gael is recycling a craft? Weaving new things around old ideas?'

'You mean this craft movement, this movement toward things hand made? Like organic farming? No, I can't see Glen returning to handknitting or weaving on any grand scale. You wouldn't make a living at it, weaving. You wouldn't make any depending on it. Just be lucky to keep it alive, that's all.

'No, I never wove for a living. Weaving is my pastime. I like messing about with thread. That's when you're your own boss. Do a half-an-hour, and a half-an-hour again. I wouldn't like to be tied down to it. Nine hours a day. A wet day, if it's raining and you've got nothing going, you go to your loom for an hour. That's the height of it'.

'The only thing recycled in Glen is wool'.
– Con O'Gara

# Rose Hegarty

I like crafts of any kind, really', said Rose Hegarty. 'I wanted to learn them all! Even if I didn't keep up with them'.

Rose, who is the aunt of Taipéis Gael's Máire McGinley, showed me a knitted black-and-white whale stuffed with wool she was making for a grandchild. 'Oh, I used to knit all kinds of ganseys', she said, using the Irish word for sweater. 'Jumpers, you know, for my children growing up. I like to experiment. I used to knit in nursing school as well. When I married, I had to give it up. But I went back to work again for a while after the kids were grown'.

Before she was married, Rose worked as a psychiatric nurse in a hospital in Letterkenny. She later had three children. She now lives with a son in Malinmore, just a mile or so from Taipéis Gael's studio. One of her daughters is married with children in Letterkenny. Another lives in London with her children.

Across the thin ribbon of road in front of her two-storey, whitewashed house, we talked while her sheep grazed inside a stone-walled pasture. Rose is a tall woman who is quick to smile. Her sheep – horned and coarse-wooled – are of the Blackface breed indigenous to the mountains of Scotland. Like a crooked path one of her ewes might take, so did our conversation leap and circle from knitting to painting to family and to sheep.

'There are other sheep behind the house on the commonage', she said, pointing behind her and away from the pasture, which overlooks the Atlantic. Rathlin O'Beirne Island gleamed. From this view it appeared as a thin sliver of land in grays and silvers that are hardly discernible from sea and sky.

Her sheep huddled into the far corner of her field as I asked her if they have always been part of her life.

'There was always sheep around, except when I was working in Letterkenny. I think just about every family here has sheep. Well it's a good place for rearing them. They were part of the livelihood down through the years. But there's too many of them now. They're overstocked in every area. They're getting nothing for them. This year was a bad year for feeding. Very wet. Hard to save any fodder for them. We do silage for them and that, you see. So you have to have the weather'.

'Silage?' I asked.

'Pasture grass. Even the sheep feeding for themselves outside – too much rain is not good for them'.

I zipped my jacket against the damp wind. 'Do you sell your sheep fleeces?'

'Yes, I do. But it wouldn't buy the clippers to clip them for what you get for wool right now. Terrible. Even the sheep – you wouldn't get a thing for the lambs. There was no such thing as selling them this year. You would only get £5 a sheep or some such thing. You just rather let them go wild and that. But seeing that you have land, you may as well have something on it. My son keeps them for me. I wouldn't have them otherwise'.

'I know what you mean. I keep a few sheep', I said.

'Have you?' her voice became animated. 'How do you manage to keep them?'

'I've only three so it's not much work, not like yours. Have you ever sheared your sheep, Rose?'

'It's not a woman's job, really. You know you have so much else to do. Now it's much easier with the electric shears and all. No, the sheep are too heavy. Maybe I would, if you could shear them standing up!'

Rose Hegarty, resident of Malinmore and aunt of Taipéis Gael artist Máire McGinley, helped the weavers with spinning and natural dye techniques when their cooperative first opened.

One of three striped tabby cats ran from her still-blooming November garden and jumped onto her sitting-room windowsill. It arched its back and rubbed against the pane. Opening the front door of her house, Rose said, 'She's like a spoiled child, she is'.

We settled into her dim but cheerful sitting room. Rose sat beside a 1940s Wamsler stove. I took a chair at a dining table by the window. Faces of grandchildren, family, and wedding photographs filled the walls and peered from frames on a small corner stand. Icons of the Blessed Mother and paintings hung together with decorative plates above an antique cupboard, where she keeps china and fluted vases.

A watercolour caught my interest, of Rose's field, the sea and Rathlin O'Beirne Island, the same scene as I saw in front of me.

'Did you paint this?' I asked.

'Ah, no. It's well done, isn't it? The fellow who used to live up the way painted it, Conal McIntyre. His brother is equally as good'. Conal McIntyre has woven for Taipéis Gael. 'I knew his family in Malinbeg. Conal was coming and going a lot. Travelling. He didn't show his paintings much. You could go over to his house and have a look.

'I do painting myself', she continued. 'They're not good. I'm only learning. But you get so . . . you know . . . engrossed in it!'

After asking to see her work, she opened her portfolio to the first watercolour. 'This is supposed to be a bog in the fall or winter'. Rose had captured the peach-rose tints of the heather in November. 'And this one's just a sunset – I like that one'.

Later, I brought my friend Marie Nordgren to meet Rose. Marie, who is a watercolourist, studied Rose's painting and said, 'You seem to be able to make a sweep with your brush and just leave it at that. I tend to keep going over and over mine until I ruin it!'

Handing Marie a book, Rose said, 'This is very helpful. It shows you step by step how to blend the colors. That's really the most important thing – the mixing of the colours'.

As Rose explained a bit about each of her paintings to Marie, my mind wandered to tapestry; how colours are blended by working two strands of a different colour together through the warp, or by *hachure* – a technique that works two strands of different colours towards each other to create a layered look. I also thought about how fortunate Taipéis Gael has been to have a colour-blending natural like Rose close at hand. Perhaps most fortunate is Rose's niece, Máire McGinley, to whom Rose has passed on her spinning and natural dyeing skills.

While turning over the last two of her paintings, Rose said, 'This is a fence. That one's a lough'.

'Is it the lough on the bogland between here and Carrick?' I asked.

'Ah, no. It's just one I made up', she said.

I found Rose's experimental nature invigorating. It is a quality to be found in many people in Glencolmcille. Undoubtedly, this dynamic creative environment helped encourage Taipéis Gael.

Rose smoothed her sweater and folded her hands in her lap. 'Sure, I knitted as a child, too. From homespun. My mother dyed the wool with heather and *crotal*, the lichens off the rocks. My brother wove tweed for Gaeltarra Éireann. We did the spinning for him. We had to be up late and early in the morning to get the things finished for market day. And, oh, we'd get the works if we didn't keep up!' She gave me a fiendish smile, as if she'd just been caught in the act of skipping her chores.

'You must be hungry', she said, getting up and walking to her kitchen. 'I'll just put together some tea and a wee bite to eat'.

As she rustled about in drawers, opened and closed cabinets, I thought of how spinning yarn from the fleece is an enormous amount of work. She and her family must have been working all the time. An average estimate of what one spinner can produce is 2 lb of yarn a day, the equivalent of eight four-ounce skeins. A medium-sized adult sweater will need 1 lb of yarn. But this does not take into consideration the hours of preparation of the fleece for spinning: picking, washing, drying and carding. As Judith Hoad noted about this era in *This is Donegal Tweeds*, it took five spinners to keep one weaver at work full time.[1]

When she came back carrying a plate of ham and cheese sandwiches, I asked, 'did you work with wool from the fleece?

'Aye, we had to take it off the sheep, break it up, oil and card it, make rolls of it, spin it, and fill the bobbins for the weavers'.

'The oil was used for what purpose?'

'We didn't wash the fleece, you see. In winter there was no way of drying it, really. We hadn't the machines we do now. The wool wouldn't spin properly without oil. We called it "sweet oil". We'd sprinkle it over the wool'.

One possible benefit of the oil would have been to cut the stickiness of the lanolin. I find if I spin a fleece that has not been washed, my hands and the wheel become gummed up. Sweet oil likely helped prevent a build up of residue.

Did you use a Donegal wheel?'

'I did. The kind Taipéis Gael has'.

Pouring us both tea, she continued. 'We used to double the thread for knitting yarn. We'd spin singles for the weft for the tweed. The warp we spun tight. The weft you could have little bobbles, you know, of colour'.

'The flecks of colour in tweed?'

'I tell you how they did it. They mixed it through the wool before they spun it. They carded it out until the wool was fine, then they sprinkled these in and then they spun it'. Rose explained that they kept some of their homespun yarn for themselves for socks and sweaters. 'I knitted for the family when I was a teenager. I made matching skirts and jumpers for the children'.

'Was anyone known locally for their expertise in spinning?' I asked.

'There was no one in particular known for their spinning. But the weavers would tell you who was good and who was bad. "You do that a bit better next time!" they'd say. Because if the threads were breaking, then it's trouble, you know. You had to remember to spin the warp one way and the weft the other. That was the combination of it, like'.

'Did you ever weave tweed yourself?' I asked.

'I'd go in and have a shot at it. I wouldn't know how to draw the thread through the heddles. They had nothing then to tell you how to do it. You had to memorize the

*Weaving Tapestry in Rural Ireland*

pattern, like the herringbone. Sometimes there would be two, three or four heddles. It took a long time. 'Twas tedious'.

After we finished our sandwiches, we drove up the winding, single-width road to Taipéis Gael's studio in the newly renovated school-house in Malinbeg. As we climbed the stairs we could hear the knitting machines from the business on the first floor 'whooshing' back and forth with a loud racket.

At the top we entered a world of wool, wheels and creativity. Tapestries of sheep-strewn headlands, Children of Lir swans and abstract designs coloured all of the walls. Bolts of blue, yellow and purple yarn crowded the floor beside the looms.

Rose seated herself at a table beside windows that overlook land and sea, a Martello Tower and the south shore of Rathlin O'Beirne Island. She poured over some of Laurence Boland's photographs that would be used for this book, and helped the tapestry artists select subjects to weave from Lar's images of ruins, rocks or kittiwake roosts. Taipéis Gael members gasped in awe at black and white prints featuring the landscape they daily inhabit. Their behaviour reminded me of someone whose blindfold has suddenly been lifted, enabling them to see their surroundings for the first time. Rose chose some for herself to paint.

My visit with Rose stretched into the evening. From the studio we walked with Máire McGinley to her house for hot whiskey. On the way Rose told us a story that reminded me again of why I admire her, and why Taipéis Gael is lucky to have a woman with such varied interests living nearby.

Her story began with her being invited to join a few friends in Innishowen for a three-day watercolour workshop, sponsored by the Irish Countrywomen's Association. Rose said, 'When I got there the painting class had been filled. But that was all right. I was up there for the fun of it and for the company. So I had a look into some of the other classes and I chose the next best thing'.

'And what was that?' I asked.

'Aromatherapy'.

This view of Rathlin O'Beirne Island is similar to the one from Rose Hegarty's home in Malinmore. The sheep in the foreground are likely of her flock. Images of the lighthouse in the distance have been woven into Taipéis Gael's tapestries. On this island, weaver Máire McGinley grazes her sheep in the summer. The locals travel there to shear them.

# Jimmy Carr

One summer evening at Monica de Bath's cottage in Glencolmcille, I met Jimmy for the first time. We had planned to go on to Roarty's pub to take in some of Glen's annual International Fiddle Festival.

A man in his eighties, I found Jimmy Carr to have the spirit and mischievous laugh of a schoolboy. He had arrived that night on a motorbike. 'You drive a motorcycle', I said.

'Aye, I do. Half a motorcycle! Have been for twenty years'. Agile as a mountain sheep, he negotiated his way up the irregular stone steps – indistinguishable in the dark from the ground around them – and through the gate to Monica's front door. I followed on unsteady feet.

Monica welcomed us with tea and toddies. A turf fire hissed quietly in the hearth. One of her early tapestries, in soft earth tones of natural dyes, warmed the whitewashed wall behind her couch, where we were seated.

'These young weavers are very great, very great', Jimmy said about Taipéis Gael. 'There's someone there to keep it all going, the carding, the dyeing, the spinning. I hate to see things die off, like so many other arts, crafts and ways of doing things – so few people making bread any more, growing their own yeast, or haying their own fields by hand. It's all a terrible, terrible lot of work'.

Jimmy glanced at the fire. I asked him about his involvement with the local tweed industry as an adolescent.

'I did a good bit with the weaving – the dyeing, carding, spinning. Not that many men spun. It was mostly the women. It was common for the men to do the carding or dyeing, but not spinning.

'My uncles wove. And the man next door was set up for weaving. I used to help them. It was an awful lot of work. The wool had to be cleaned, dyed, spun. You'd dye the wool first, before you'd spin it'.

'Did you use the Donegal wheel, the kind Taipéis Gael uses now?'

'Aye. We used it for spinning warp, the Donegal wheel. This wheel was originally made for spinning flax, but we used it for wool. And there was a big wheel, it was much higher', he raised his hand above his head. 'We used it for filling shuttle bobbins for weft thread'.

We talked a bit about the use of flax in this part of Donegal. Jimmy explained, 'Flax was used way back in 1914, even earlier. People didn't grow it here much. Maybe the land wasn't suited. There's a lot of it growing near Kilmecranan, County Tyrone. Up north. Good bit of it growing for thatching and that sort of stuff. I use it to thatch my own roof. Like weaving, it's very hard work!'

'Tell me how tweed yarn was prepared', I said, sipping my tea as Monica sat down to join us.

'For tweed, the warp was spun to right. And the weft, to the left. If the weaver had bad warp, it'd take him ages to weave a web of 50 to 80 yards. He'd make very little money. There were many stories about spinners who spun poor weft for weavers they didn't like. The yarn would break again and again on the weaver!

'Warping for a web weighed about 50–75 lb on the beam'.

Monica explained to me that the beam is a round post that runs the width of the back of the loom to which the warp threads are attached. As the fabric grows, the weaver winds it around the beam.

'Aye, you'd twist and twist!' Jimmy said, shaking his head.

'How are the flecks of colour woven in to the tweed?' I asked.

Jimmy Carr used to help his uncles with the tweed weaving – carding, spinning and dyeing wool. He and Monica de Bath drove all over Glencolmcille and beyond in search of people who remembered the traditional methods of local textile work to find possible mentors for Taipéis Gael.

'For the tweeds, what they used to do is mix a third black wool with two-thirds white wool. That's for warp. And then for weft, they used two-thirds black wool. And that was expensive. Black yarn was dyed with logwood and a copper mordant. The logwood came from Africa'.

Jimmy recalled, without hesitation, on which days – over fifty years ago – weavers brought their goods to market. 'The first of every month, we sold at the Ardara market, the 14th in Carrick, 26th in Kilcar. We went there by pony and cart or walked. All day market. There was a fair amount of competition. There would be about three, four hundred pieces of tweed there. About every house would bring 40 to 80 yards'.

Occasionally there might be a contest at a fair where contestants formed teams of shearers, carders, spinners and knitters. Similar 'sheep to shawl' competitions are held in the United States at sheep and wool gatherings. But Jimmy didn't have a specific name for these festivities in Donegal. 'There were men in Glencolmcille who could card to beat the band!' Jimmy laughed and added that he didn't much like the games, 'I used to try to get away. Aye, aye'.

'Jimmy, what is it like to work with hundreds of sheep?' I asked, telling him that I keep three of my own in a barn. He laughed at this – that I keep only three sheep, and fenced in, no less. In Glencolmcille, the flocks enjoy free rein of the land: they perch on cliffs overlooking the sea; lie in the road chewing their cud; or lean against cottages beneath window boxes, like a pet dog might.

'I've got sheep. Sell them usually for meat. So many lambs. The wool isn't even worth thirteen pence a pound. These days I'm putting up a fence to keep them out. It's a very hard job! The posts and wires and all that sort of thing'. He chuckled.

'My sheep are mostly Blackface, but there are some Cheviot, too. There are a few Suffolks about. Very fine wool. They didn't use it in the tweeds. But in Dundee, in the north of Scotland, and in the east of Scotland, they used it for worsted (tightly spun) yarns. Lovely dark blues'.

Jimmy said that sheep are sheared once a year in Glencolmcille. 'June or July, weather permitting. You can't shear 'em if they're wet, you see'.

Jimmy explained that the locals splash red, blue and green water-soluble paint on the backs of their flocks to help determine which belong to whom.

'But I've seen multicoloured marks on some', I said. 'How do you remember from year to year which colour belongs to whom?' The question unearthed a story from Jimmy's childhood about a neighbour who found walnuts and decided to brew them into a dye for wool.

'The walnuts made a thick brown solution, which he liked. So he branded his lambs that spring walnut brown. The fellow assumed the colour would wash out because the wool on the sheep's backs hadn't been mordanted first – a step in the dye process that

Jimmy Carr helping
Máire McGinley with
warp thread.

bonds dye with wool. But what he didn't know was that walnuts are one of the few dye materials that do not require a mordant. The dye took to the wool and never faded! The following spring, on market-day, he found himself madly cutting out the brown sections of all his fleeces! Aye, he didn't get much for his wool that year'.

Rounding up sheep for shearing is done a number of ways. One method still used today in Glencolmcille is to run them, perhaps with a border collie, into an abandoned structure or crush. Often these are ruins of stonewalls or dilapidated famine houses. Both Jimmy and Taipéis Gael weaver Dermot Cannon have used the ruined houses in Port, a deserted, pre-Famine village about eleven miles from Glencolmcille, where only a few homes are occupied today.

I told Jimmy about my visit to the famine houses in Port and how I had thought they might be used as crushes when I saw that the windows had been rocked-in and splattered with red paint. I had also found a twig covered with red paint embedded in a crack in the stonework, which looked like a paint-stirring stick. White locks of wool beneath my feet shimmered in the sun that day on the wet grass.

Jimmy said, 'The windows and doors need to be barricaded so that when you run the sheep into the structure, they can't leap out the other side. People sometimes build circular walls in the middle of an open field with available rocks if there are no empty structures nearby'.

Jimmy Carr preparing wool for Taipéis Gael weaver Dermot Cannon to spin.

'One wonders if the slubs in the yarns of Donegal homespun tweed originated as a result of poor carding and have since been retained as a tradition and a mark of authenticity'. – M.L. Ryder, *Sheep and Man.*

'A good homespun differs from factory yarn as does an illuminated page of a manuscript differ from a page of print'. – T.W. Rolleston, *Ireland Industrial.*

Jimmy Carr making a rolag, a tube-like cloud of wool which is then spun into thread.

'You obviously enjoyed the weaving part of your life. You seem to look back on it fondly, even though it was work', I said.

'That's exactly what it was'. He laughed, swilled the last of his tea, and looked into the bottom of his glass. 'Hard work'.

I came to know Jimmy Carr a bit more with each visit to Glencolmcille and each letter or Christmas card exchanged. His commitment to community runs deep and his devotion to Taipéis Gael is unfailing. His appreciation of wool seems fathomless and perhaps this can only be understood by people who work with sheep or create with their fleeces.

In the fall of 1998, Jimmy attended a Taipéis Gael workshop in which the participants (weavers, knitters, textile designers and a horticulturist) gathered to broaden their knowledge of the old natural dye recipes. Jimmy's memory nudged the group along. He helped to identify plants and seaweed and to fill in the gaps in scant dye records.

After the workshop, Jimmy parked his motorbike on the kerb next to my car, beside a local market. He grinned when I found for him – among the wool and dyepots, books and backpacks in my trunk – one lustrous skein of yarn dyed silver-green with bog sludge.

'Lovely!' he said, holding it into the blue of the sky that morning. 'Lovely', he said again, shaking his head slightly to the right. I don't believe in that instance that his reaction was only about the colour. As Henry Glassie wrote in *The Spirit of Folk Art*, 'As artists we stand humbly before all of the past'. [2] Beside the market that fine morning, both Jimmy and this little skein of wool said as much.

As well as being a mentor to Taipéis Gael, Jimmy Carr is a community leader. 'All down the years', said handknitter Bríd McGlenchey, 'Jimmy's been helping with projects in Glen. He's very good, you know. He leads heritage tours for Oideas Gael, Glencolmcille's cultural college'.

The college's founder and administrator, Liam Ó Cuinneagáin, said, 'Jimmy is the most dependable, reliable man I know. He has a huge respect for native culture and language. And yet he's a private man. He hasn't a phone. To get in touch with him it often takes going through several people – even the President doesn't have a buffer that deep'.

Mary McNelis, owner of Rossan Sweater Factory attested, 'I'm sure nobody has a bad word for Jimmy. He lives way up; he's probably five miles or more from church, the shops and everything. And he comes down to meet the American coaches that come here to Oideas Gael. He greets the visitors and takes them all around the parish and then to the megalithic tomb here in Malinmore. He tells them all about the pre-Christian monuments. He's very much into tradition. He's marvellous, he really is'.

Jimmy has been host to musicians from all over the world. 'He doesn't get much sleep, does he?' said Rose Hegarty, 'The musicians all know him at this stage. They are fortunate to have him to show them around'.

He's spoken at cultural events around the country, including a huge benefit sponsored by the Office of Public Works and the Crafts and Heritage Council in Dublin, at which Taipéis Gael weavers debuted their work. According to Monica de Bath, 'Jimmy followed with a speech longer and more eloquent than the Minister'.

Jimmy leads *An Turas,* a pilgrimage in the footsteps of St Colmcille. In 1955, Daphine Mound reported that the pilgrimage was the longest surviving pilgrimage in Ireland. It is a pilgrimage that is performed formally and informally through the summer months, alone or with family and friends. It takes about three to five hours to travel its fifteen stations.

Local lore holds that *An Turas* is led by the saint himself, who cuts a path through the valleys. Yet Liam Ó Cuinneagáin qualifies this belief, 'Jimmy Carr single-handedly keeps the tradition of the St Colmcille pilgrimage alive. He even trims back briars and rakes the way for better access before pilgrims arrive'.

As Father Peoples of Glencolmcille Parish once said, 'I wish I were as holy as Jimmy Carr'.

Describing *An Turas* to me in a letter, Jimmy said, 'I will guide any people who come here to do it. The walk is three miles long, twenty-four things in all: St Colmcille's bed, a wishing stone, a chair, a well, a boat, an altar and a place of the knees. Walked in the bare feet, we start a torch-light procession at twelve o'clock on the 8th of June and walk through the night finishing around day clear'.

This account of the pilgrimage would not be complete without mention of the sensory details the participants experience, such as those reported by the students, visitors and the staff of Oideas Gael and Taipéis Gael, who have had the privilege of walking the pattern with Jimmy. A four-time participant, Dr Eileen Moore Quinn recalled, 'The exhilarating coldness of the grass, the sting of nettles and barbed wire, the urge to wriggle my toes in the soft mud as I sat in the saint's chair'.

Taipéis Gael weaver Margaret Cunningham recalled a story Jimmy Carr tells about it being St Colmcille who kept him from emigrating to America. 'Jimmy had planned to go one spring, saved up for the passage, but he'd broken his foot on the pilgrimage. He understood that as Divine intervention'.

In a letter to me, Jimmy elaborated. 'I did not break my foot on the *Turas.* I broke it at home and I was going around with two crutches. I thought I would do the *Turas* anyway and when I left the station with the chair, I did not want the crutch. I had not a pain in the foot from that day to this. As I did not get off the doctor's books for two years, I could not go to America. Maybe that's the way things were meant to be, as I have helped lots of people do the *Turas* since'.

Jimmy Carr at a station along *An Turas*, the local pilgrimage.

Station Fifteen of the local pilgrimage, *An Turas*, which was often led by Jimmy Carr. Note the interlacing design in 'mansucript tradition' on the standing stone, as archaeologist Michael Herity describes the pillar stones in this area.

*Cloch An Aonach,*
Stone of the
Gatherings (detail),
Máire McGinley.

See p.114 for
full image.

Photographer Laurence Boland walked the pilgrimage route privately with Jimmy Carr. On this particular day, Jimmy carried a type of divining rod given to him by a German geologist. 'I don't show this to most people', he told Laurence.

'What's it for?'

'Finding ruins under the sod. Would you like to give it a try?' Jimmy handed Laurence the copper stick.

Laurence later told me that when he held it, it wouldn't quiver for him even a hair's width, but it worked magic when Jimmy held it.

What Jimmy has found or not found with his copper rod is his secret. But if ever there is such a thing as divining for stone, I believe Jimmy Carr could do it. We've talked about stone and what it is like to live with so much of it. Something about the light in his eyes and his tone of voice led me to believe that he finds holiness in anything that lasts, including rock. He informed me that in Glencolmcille there is 'granite, whinstone, limestone, green slab stone, quartz, and a type of white marble. The first five of these are for building houses and sheds, walls and stone ditches. Limestone can be broken up and burned in lime kilns and it's great fertilizer for gardens, meadow, or grazing land. All these stones are used for making roads and bridges, quartz or granite being the hardest, green slab and limestone the softest'.

Perhaps his fascination with rocks coincided with his early interest in the archaeology and history of the area. 'There is a lot of this around both land and sea'. According to Jimmy, Colmcille 'blessed the clay that can be lifted from under the saint's bed, or at the wishing-stone or the altar'. He said, 'No one who has it will get killed by lightning; a house it's kept in will never get burned, and in a boat that keeps it, nobody will drown'.

As schist makes up the bulk of the pre-Christian standing stones, court tombs and crude Christian altars of *An Turas* (Colmcille's bed, chair and the like), would it be a stretch to believe that Jimmy Carr – keeper of this tradition and a man who makes maps of grass and stone, who prays with his feet, and who thinks with the landscape – is indeed, by way of his divining rod, privy to sites that may still lie hidden beneath the turf?

Land and sea – both mountainous in Glencolmcille at times, depending on the wind – are the geographical and sacred contours of Jimmy Carr's homeland. He honours and shares them with anyone who seeks his guidance. 'People are left with a tremendous sense of reverence for him and the place', Liam Ó Cuinneagáin said.

Jimmy Carr drinking
from St Colmcille's
Well, Station Seven
of *An Turas*. Pilgrims
bring three stones
up the hill to this
well in the townland
of Beefan. Walking
around the well three
times, they leave
a stone at each go
round. Afterwards, it
is customary to drink
from the well and
to take some water
home.

# Administrator of Taipéis Gael, Annie McGinley

Annie McGinley is the youngest of twelve children, who were all born and raised in Glencolmcille. After leaving secondary school she moved to Dublin to work for a number of years in a Russian/Scandinavian restaurant while taking a secretarial course. She lived in France as an au-pair, and became fluent in the French language. She speaks fluent Irish as well. She eventually moved back to Donegal where she settled. She has a son, Oisín, who is in secondary school. She is involved with the local youth club and the Sliabh Liag Athletic Club.

Annie has a great appreciation of art in all its forms, and has travelled in Europe and the US. 'I love learning about different cultures and the way people live.'

It is inside Annie McGinley's office where Taipéis Gael's mission statement, 'Weaving a Future from Our Past', becomes apparent. As I knocked on the glass window of her office door in the old Malinbeg school, I found Annie dressed in a sweater and pair of jeans, seated at a computer, updating the cooperative's web page. A seventeenth-century model of a spinning wheel stood beside me. Both are tools of her trade.

Ten years ago when Taipéis Gael formed its cooperative, they didn't own a computer, only the spinning wheel. 'I can't imagine any business managing without a computer at this stage. The internet has helped us keep up with what's going on in the world of fibre arts. The weavers benefit from looking at other artists' work and showing their own.' Annie spoke loudly to be heard over the roar of rain on the studio's metal roof. She moved a stack of files off a chair and offered me a seat.

'Have you sold any tapestries from the website?' I asked.

'Not as yet, but we have had queries about commissioned work. Our sales mostly come from personal contacts, from people visiting our gallery, from articles people read about us in magazines, or from exhibitions and workshops. Word of mouth is our best marketing tool, and a lot of our customers are repeat. But the internet has been wonderful in other ways – such as with correspondence overseas, which is relatively inexpensive. It's been helpful to the weavers for sending images to people who have commissioned work.'

Annie sees herself as the one among the group whose job is to reach out to the world in different ways, especially through technology. Given their rural location she feels it is essential. 'We've posted our workshops on-line; they are an important part of our business.'

In many ways the computer is a tool used in preventing emigration to larger cities or abroad. It allows these artists to work where they do – in their small corner of Donegal – yet remain connected to the world.

'One of the reasons I accepted this position is that I feel like I am doing something worthwhile. Having lived in France and more recently Letterkenny, I appreciate my home in Glencolmcille, the art and craft of the area. So do the weavers. While their tapestries depart from the old ways of tweed-making, they are keeping the tradition of weaving alive here. It is a hard thing to do. But they believe in what they are doing so much that they don't leave. It is nice to work with people of that frame of mind.

'It feels good to be setting up something in a place where you are from. Often I meet artists from different areas and their work isn't about where they're from. I'm not saying there is anything wrong with that, or that it takes anything away from their art,

Annie McGinley in the loft at Oideas Gael Cultural College, home of Taipéis Gael's first studio. Her business savvy embodies the theme of Margaret Cunningham's tapestry on the following page – *Time Warp* – as Annie is as proficient with a spinning wheel as she is navigating the internet. In her office, the word 'web' takes on a double meaning. As a child, she would have understood it as eighty yards of tweed.

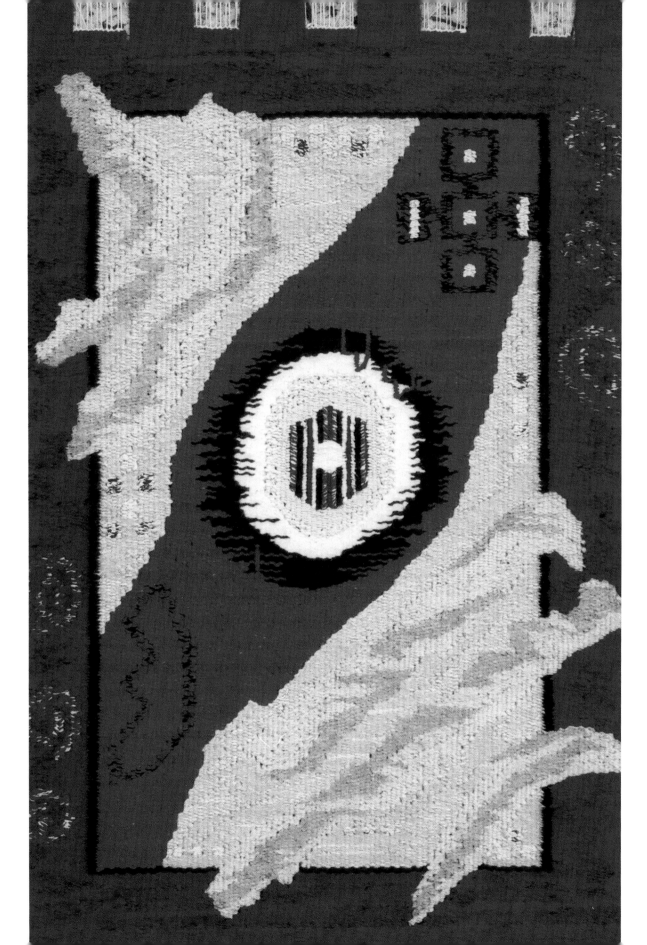

Ag Dul Siar In Am,
Time Warp, Margaret
Cunningham, 28"x
36", commercial and
handspun yarns.

Collection of Údarás
Na Gaeltachta, Barna,
County Galway

Photo: Margaret
Cunningham

it's just that it reinforces how much our work is true to place. I think we connect with people because they see the passion we have for our home in our work. I think people can appreciate this because so many other communities have lost this.'

'Do you think that your customers, or those who come for your weaving workshops, recognize this? What draws them to you?' I asked.

Annie waited for the clatter of water overhead to quiet. 'It's interesting. Some of the people who come for workshops often have some connection or affinity for this place or for fibre art or have learned about us through Oideas Gael or have friends who live in Glen. Others have no previous connections here, but stumble upon us by serendipity. Those who buy tapestries seem to identify strongly with a certain piece, with the area, or they bring their personal stories to it. They seem to understand who we are.'

'Did you experience any initial challenges when you came to work for Taipéis Gael?' I asked.

'I responded to an advertisement that simply stated that they needed an office person with computer skills. But I wound up involved in an internationally connected arts cooperative, which demanded much more than I knew! I took courses in business management, administration, marketing and sales through Údarás na Gaeltachta, for which I received certificates. I learned how to make business and marketing plans. We have two patrons, so to speak: students who come to learn weaving and customers who come to buy our artwork. In most cases they are two very different groups.

'It's a difficult thing to sell art. But working as a cooperative the weavers have advantages. Having a business manager allows them to weave while I worry about selling, organizing exhibitions, workshops, etc. I don't think selling should be in the backs of their minds as they design their next tapestry. It's an ongoing conflict – should we weave what we think might sell, or what we want to weave? You lose something in a piece if your heart's not in it.'

Muffled music from the radio the weavers had turned on in the other room filled in the lulls between rain showers.

'How have things changed, for better or worse, since your relocation from under the eaves at Oideas Gael, the cultural college in Glen, to here?'

'It feels right here. Where we are now, in the old school-house, the locals come to participate. Some of them helped to renovate it. Father Eddie Gallagher secured the funding for it. We have workshops with the local schoolchildren, which is great craic for all.'

'Has this move to a more remote location cost you any customers or students for your workshops?' I leaned an elbow on the desk behind me. Like most other creative people's desks it is a clutter of material and tools related to their art: slides, yarn, tapestry samples and sketches.

A Napoleonic signal
tower on a Malinbeg
promontory opposite
Rathlin O'Beirne
Island. Built between
1804–1806.

*Tur Martello*, Martello Tower, Sandra Mockler, 30"x48", handspun and natural dyes. This tapestry of a Napoleonic-era signal tower was one of Sandra's first, woven during the two-year training course for Taipéis Gael. Such towers rise from promontories jutting out into the sea along the western coast of Ireland.

Private collection

Photo: Margaret Cunningham

'We are a bit off the beaten path, but we are near a few sites that tourists like to go to such as the Silver Strand and Martello Tower.' Annie pointed to the ruins outside the window. 'We still get customers from Oideas Gael and some of our work hangs there. But when they arrive here in Malinbeg, we know they've come because they are interested in our work and in tapestry weaving. It is affirming of what we do.'

Their present studio is situated some 300 metres up from the sea, with large windows looking out over grazing sheep, the island and the tower. It is an ideal place for weavers to gather inspiration from the landscape. The grass, the sky and the waves never have the same pattern, due to the ever-changing light and wind.

'What kind of projects are you and Taipéis Gael currently involved in or working toward?'

'We'd like to continue teaching and exhibiting in the US and abroad. I hope the cooperative becomes very well known in Ireland and within the art world as well. We've found that it works well to give workshops at the local weaving guilds in the towns where we've been invited to exhibit. They have always responded favourably to our classes. And we hope to foster new links with other artists. One way we plan to do this is through the Denmark European Tapestry Forum. Its members are from different countries and it promotes tapestry through travelling exhibitions and a presence on the internet. This group aims to reduce isolation for individual artists.

'During the school year we give back to our own community, offer the young people more exposure to art and the business of it.' Annie reaches for photographs of the recent workshop they held for local schoolchildren that showed little hands and smiling faces at work. 'Art classes are not offered in the schools so the students aren't getting a feel for it. They wouldn't be exposed to tapestry if it weren't for Taipéis Gael. The cooperative is a great way in which the community can help itself and be proud of itself. All the material we use is grown or supplied locally. In a way it shows the students there is something worthwhile about the place they live, even though it doesn't come with a Nike brand on it.'

'Do you think Taipéis Gael serves as a model for the development of other local businesses?'

'Yes, of course. We've created something of beauty using only local products, such as wool, by using our skills and imagination, and the end result brings pleasure to people for years to come. It's a saleable product, and one that will be

exhibited widely in the area and even abroad. Our community could perhaps develop enterprises selling organic meat and vegetables or other food products such as jams. These could be sold to local restaurants and bed-and-breakfasts. More locally grown businesses would give the feeling that the community cares for and appreciates what is on our own doorstep.'

'I would think this would be attractive to tourists as well. People seek holistic experiences and appreciate eating local cuisine when they are travelling.'

'Aye, in many ways Taipéis Gael is doing its part for the environment; recycling. We use 100 per cent natural products. Wool is biodegradable. We are not energy-intensive in any way. People like to visit us and be a part of it, create something indigenous. This is how things change. Each individual or business doing their own small bit.'

'Other than these socially responsible ideas, what other advice might you give to artists who wish to start up a cooperative?'

'The cooperative form of enterprise has worked really well for us, because each artist

Silver Strand, tucked beneath Slieve League, is a short walk from Taipéis Gael's studio in Malinbeg.

was given their own creative space. Nothing was dictated. But my advice would be to be very clear at the outset as to why the group is coming together in the first place and make out a plan with measurable objectives – such as how often exhibitions will take place, pricing formulas, who is responsible for what aspects of the marketing, workshops and other related activities. Discuss everything at length beforehand.'

'What, if any, would be your advice to development agencies who give seed-money for cooperatives such as Taipéis Gael?'

'Listen to what local people are saying and trying to achieve. Give them every encouragement to give it a go, even if it only means employing two people, because that is two more people who want to stay in an economically disadvantaged area and will contribute to it. Maybe down the road those two people will employ two more people. Taipéis Gael began with a grant. At one time it employed as many as six. Over the last ten years those six attracted many dozens of workshop participants who travelled to Glen and stayed for a week or more, utilizing bed-and-breakfasts, restaurants, and the like. Some enrolled in other classes at Oideas Gael. I think it is important to give the entrepreneurs financial, technical and moral support. They will be the ones who keep the Gaeltacht from turning into a barren landscape, a wasteland that is very capable of sustaining itself. It's about national priorities, really. I think the policy-makers today could do better in this respect. You can't get better than small businesses, owned locally by people who care about the area and know the land and their own locality intimately. People who want to stay and build their communities.'

The rain hammering on the roof had yet to let up. Whitecaps raged around Rathlin O'Beirne Island, and the bone-chilling cold felt more like a January day than late March. It was nearly time for tea and to warm our hands on the radiator in the other room, but I had one last question for Annie. 'What would you say has been one of your most memorable moments in tapestry or working for Taipéis Gael?'

'When the artist sells a piece', she answered with no hesitation. 'It's reality; this business can't survive without revenue. But more than that it is a vote of confidence for the weavers and the cooperative. It motivates us all to keep at it.

'I also enjoy our workshops, the people I meet who come to learn tapestry. The relaxed atmosphere here, I think, helps them learn easily. They go away proud of what they've woven.'

'How about you, do you have a tapestry on the loom?' I asked.

'Aye, though it's been there untouched for a long while. I haven't a minute for it.'

Annie works full-time, is a mother and also a member of a local theatre group. Just last night she appeared in *Oíche Cheol Agus Drámaíochta*, a production performed in Irish. She played the role of Nora, a rebellious child who refuses to speak Irish to her parents at home. An artist in her own right, like many others in her community, Annie is an inspiration to Taipéis Gael.

# Weavers

*An Cailín Gaelach*, The
Irish Girl (Self Portrait),
Margaret Cunningham,
24"x 28", commercial
yarn. 'For this tapestry,
I wanted to work in
black and white. The
background is woven
in a diamond pattern
that I had learned
in Denmark, which
gives the piece added
texture. I wove it
sideways on the loom
to accommodate for
the straight lines and
to avoid many joins.
I've added white silk
for a bit of contrast to
the wool.

'My music, song
and weaving are
interwoven in my
life. The music is
represented by
the guitar, and my
spinning, weaving and
dyeing is depicted
by a tapestry weaver
and by the finished
tapestry on the left
side of this piece.
A large onion peel,
used for yellow dye,
is rather abstractly
drawn in the upper
left. In the center of
the piece, a weaver
looking out the
window at a tree
is singing. I played
guitar before I learned
to weave. This gave
me confidence that I
would one day master
this craft as I did the
guitar. I knew I had to
give myself time.'

Collection of Margaret
Cunningham

Photo: Margaret
Cunningham

# Margaret Cunningham

Margaret Cunningham was born in the village of Carrick, about ten kilometres from Glencolmcille, where she was raised with two brothers and a sister. Her parents Rita and Charlie were very supportive of her endeavours in both music and art. Her father recently passed away, though Margaret says, 'His love and encouragement of me as a daughter, artist and musician will live on forever'.

After studying science for two years at the regional college in Letterkenny, Margaret joined Taipéis Gael. She describes her experience with the weaving cooperative as a privilege, which not only helped her grow artistically, but as a person. She says that her co-weavers have become friends for life.

As well as being a weaver, Margaret is well established in the world of Irish music and was lead singer in the band Na Dorsa, that has just released a CD.

*Harley Davidson*,
Margaret Cunningham,
10" x 14", commercial
yarn. Jimmy Carr isn't
the only one in Glen
fond of motorcycles.
Margaret wove this
piece after a visit
to her relative's
motorcycle club in
New York. She's since
been commissioned
by other biking
enthusiasts for
tapestries of their own
cycles.

Collection of A.
Turkington

Photo: Margaret
Cunningham

*Tuilleadh Eisc*, An
Abundance of Fish,
Margaret Cunningham,
33"x43", commercial
yarns. Woven in
celebration of the
fishing tradition,
which plays an
important role in the
lives of Glencolmcille
locals today. 'After
our workshop with
Danish weavers, I
used the vertical
soumac technique I
had learned for the
fish skeletons. It made
the work more three-
dimensional'.

Collection of Knock
Airport, Knock, Ireland

Photo: Taipéis Gael

*Celtic Sunset*,
Margaret Cunningham,
24"x24", commercial
yarn. 'This sunset
scene on Teelin Bay
denotes a fairy fort
in the foreground
– the one I recall from
my childhood on the
Kilcar side of the bay.
The white and blue
interlace on the dark
brown depicts the
wee streams carving
through the sand when
the tide is out'.

Collection of Knock
Airport, Knock, Ireland

Photo: Margaret
Cunningham

*Ugly Duckling*, Dermot Cannon, 24"x 42", handspun and natural dyes.

Collection of Údarás na Gaeltachta, Barna, County Galway

Photo: Dermot Cannon

# Dermot Cannon

Dermot Cannon was born and raised in Glencolmcille and has lived in this community all his life. His interests include drawing, painting, reading and various sporting activities including hill-walking. He breeds his own Scottish Blackfaced mountain sheep.

As a tapestry artist he has been involved with group exhibitions in Europe and the US, which 'broadened my outlook and brought many new influences to my work'. He is currently working in a stone quarry near his home.

*Bare Trees*, Dermot
Cannon, 30"x30",
commercial and
handspun yarn.

Collection of Taipéis
Gael

Photo: Annie McGinley

*Ag Seoltoireacht*,
Sailing, Dermot
Cannon, 30"x48",
commercial yarn.
'The waters near
Malinbeg and Teelin in
Glencolmcille – with
their rugged coastline
and nestled harbours
– are ideal for sailing'.

Collection of Peter
Hooper

Photo: Margaret
Cunningham

*Ar Mo Bhealach Abhaile*, Homeward Bound, Dermot Cannon, 46"x 36", commercial yarn. 'A lot of my work captures the colours and shapes and images in the land and sea here'.

Collection of Mary Ann Hawrylak

Photo: Margaret Cunningham

*Teach Ceanntuí*, Thatched Cottage, Dermot Cannon, 48"x 30", natural dyes and handspun yarn. Thatched homes and hand-raked silage still thrive in Glencolmcille. 'This piece was one of my early tapestries and woven without a cartoon. I improvised as I went. The tree has no leaves because it was too hard for me to weave leaves at the time. I remember feeling good about the work as a whole when finished; the composition and movement came together'.

Collection of Ann Ueltschi

Photo: Ann Ueltschi

*An Uaig*, The Harbour,
Máire McGinley, 30"x
30", natural dyes and
handspun yarn. This
image is based on
views of Malinbeg.
Máire wove silk into
the piece for added
shimmer and texture.

Collection of Mrs.
Antonis

Photo: Máire McGinley

# Máire McGinley

Máire McGinley was born in a small thatched cottage in Glencolmcille in 1949. The second of eight children, she credits her mother with teaching her how to sew at an early age. She learned on a Singer foot machine, her mother's most prized possession. At age sixteen, she received an honours certificate in advanced needlework from a technical school. In 1993, after having raised six children with her husband Conell, and having spent over twenty years working in the home, she joined Taipéis Gael. 'I enjoyed working with the wonderful youthful group', she says, 'and I know my life has been enriched so much by the whole experience'.

Examples of Máire's explorations in Celtic art and shapes.

Photo: Taipéis Gael

Máire's sketch for a piece based on *Colmcille* (see page 107).

Photo: Taipéis Gael

Right: Máire's sketches for *Salmon Leap.*

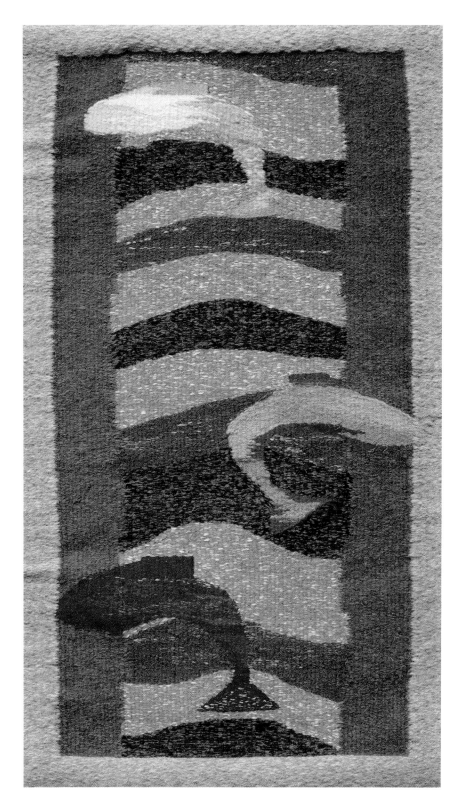

*Léim an Bhradáin*, Salmon Leap, Máire McGinley, 30"x42", handspun and commercial yarns. A piece that recalls the catch from the nearby sea. 'Salmon signifies wisdom. The warm peach colours made me think of salmon. The perimeter is woven with very thick manufactured thread, and the salmon are panels set into the border'.

Collection of Father McKee, St Joseph's Church, Beltsville, Maryland

Photo: Máire McGinley

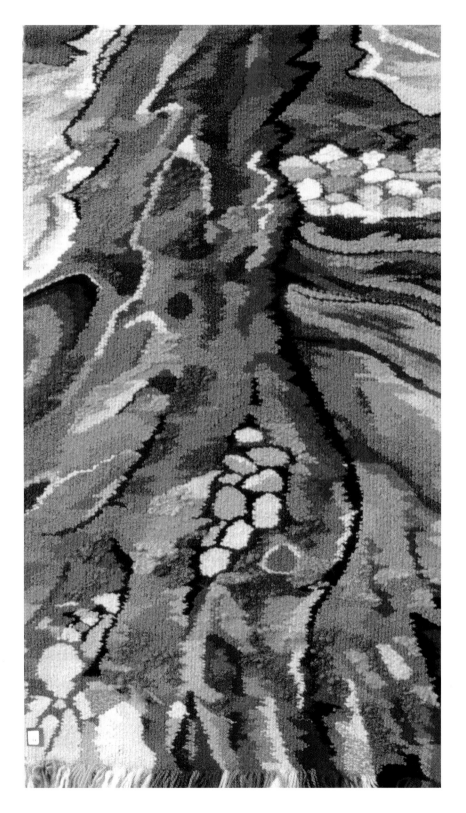

*Landscape Impressions*, Conal McIntyre, 20"x 30", commercial and handspun yarn. 'I used quite a bit of handspun in this tapestry. Because the homespun wool was rather clotted, the tension wasn't spread evenly and it didn't hang well in the end. But I like its vibrancy'.

Collection of Judy Lydon

Photo: Conal McIntyre

# Conal McIntyre

Conal McIntyre was born and raised in Malinbeg, on the coast road out of Glencolmcille. He was educated at St Eunan's College, sixty miles away, where he boarded for five years. It was there that he received his first formal art instruction. 'Later I attended the Limerick School of Art to pursue an art teacher's certificate. I also studied at Putney School of Art in London. I worked in graphic design for a Christian group for a number of years.

'I travelled to Africa where I taught, painted and sketched. While working in Sudan I married Heather and with the arrival of our two sons we decided to move back to Ireland. It was then that I joined Taipéis Gael and worked in tapestry for two years. I have since completed a purpose built studio and gallery in my garden and am back to painting again'.

*Rocks*, Conal McIntyre, 20" x 30", commercial yarn. 'In this piece I am drawing on colours and form in nature with an eye for movement'.

Collection of Sam Couch

Photo: Conal McIntyre

*In The Eye Of The Ocean*, Conal McIntyre, 28"x 48", commercial yarn. 'This was the second tapestry I wove. I'm chasing movement here. I used shapes from the sea: waves, weed, fish. I am accustomed to painting and how a paintbrush can achieve fluid lines. With weaving, it's much harder; the structure of warp and weft stifles this. And when you hammer down a section of weft with your fingers, you discover you've lost that sweep'.

Collection of Patricia Maloney

Photo: Conal McIntyre

# Conversations with the Weavers

AUTHOR: In 2005 Taipéis Gael celebrated its official tenth anniversary, although you actually came together two years before this. What is the secret of your success?

MÁIRE: We ask ourselves that everyday!

MARGARET: I think the fact that we all wanted to stay here has helped us invest ourselves in the cooperative.

DERMOT: We wanted to make something of the work and the grant and the course we completed. I think at the end of the training we knew if we didn't continue we'd never come back to it.

 I think also for me, I've the responsibility for our family's sheep. It would be hard to drive to a job far from here and maintain the farm.

MARGARET: Seven years ago, I never would have dreamed of achieving what we have. I think that helps keep us going. I wouldn't have dreamed of exhibiting in America and Europe, teaching courses, being interviewed on television for our work.

MÁIRE: You forget how far you've come until someone shows up from Japan for a tapestry class or someone wants to write an article or book about you. Especially having come from a place where no art was offered in school.

MARGARET: I think the most encouragement came when someone sold the first piece. I remember thinking, 'My God, someone sold one!' We are never vexed if someone sells more tapestries than the other. I think we share a deep sense of appreciation for each other and our work.

What are the benefits of working as a group besides that it is easier for a group to pull together enough tapestries for an exhibition?

MARGARET: I think working as a cooperative is the secret to our success so far. Foremost, we feed off each other's inspiration. We have varied strengths and tastes, which is good because we learn from each other: Dermot enjoys spinning and keeps us supplied with homespun; Máire draws well and she has an interest in the natural dyes; Annie – we are so fortunate to have her – reaches our customers in a creative way. The administration side of this business would otherwise keep us from weaving and frustrate us in many ways.

MÁIRE: Cooperatives suit artists in a way that gives them freedom to focus on just the art. Sure, we all help Annie with the marketing and selling to some extent, and we all have an equal say in decisions. But she allows us more time for tapestry.

DERMOT: Working with others is a strong motivating factor. There's a social aspect to a cooperative. You aren't alone at home weaving.

What have been some of your professional hurdles, personally or as a group?

MARGARET: I think one of the first professional hurdles for us was the completion of our two-year training course and gaining a National Certificate, as none of us had prior art schooling. The next hurdle was whether or not to form Taipéis Gael after we finished the training course that Monica de Bath had arranged for us. This is when we lost Sandra Mockler and Angela Byrne.

**Why did they leave?**

MARGARET: They needed a steady income, something the cooperative couldn't offer. Sandra went to work for Mary McNelis' sweater outlet. Angela left for England.

I felt a commitment to go on. The grant was awarded for this purpose – to build a business.

For me personally, the first hurdle was selling my first piece which I suppose was about two years into my weaving. But it wasn't until I received my first commission that I really felt I had reached a professional level, when people believed in me to design and weave a piece – from my own imagination – that was to be significant to them.

MÁIRE: Aye. Dealing with commissions was a mental hurdle for me because suddenly you are involved with others' thought processes. It's often a collaboration in coming up with a design.

I also agree with the initial hurdles our group faced that Margaret mentioned. After the two-year course we had to decide whether to stick with it or not. Knowing that Horizons and Údarás na Gaeltachta had put thousands of pounds into it, I couldn't imagine letting the skills go to waste. It's like a person, Taipéis Gael; it would be difficult to just walk away.

DERMOT: I think when members of the art community buy, commission or ask us to exhibit, it is validation that we have reached a professional level in our work. It sends a stronger message than when a tourist buys a piece. I think it was Margaret's piece, *Utah*, which sold to the Chief County Librarian in Letterkenny, who is also the Public Art Buyer for the County Council.

MARGARET: Aye. And the fellow in New York, Joseph Murphy, the art collector who commissioned all the Famine tapestries.

MÁIRE: I think, also, the fact that we receive travel grants offered by the Irish Arts Council and Aer Lingus speaks to our professionalism. What we do is considered deserving of their funds.

DERMOT: And we've invitations to several Irish festivals, some in America. The first was early on, during our two-year course, to Milwaukee. Others in Florida and Seattle. We've been in others in Ireland as well.

## INFLUENCES FROM THE LANDSCAPE

**I recall one of Angela Byrne's early tapestries with earthy hues depicting a turf cart below Mount Errigal. Do you draw inspiration from images and colours of your surroundings?**

DERMOT: Ah, you might see nice scenery. Take notice of it. It would be the landscape. But then a lot of it would be capturing the texture and warmth of the colours too. I like to use the natural colours for landscapes such as when I am weaving rocks – to tie it all together.

I wouldn't look at a sheep the same way again. I set aside about twelve fleeces for spinning each year after shearing. Even the locals bring us a nice fleece now and then. We'd be the only people in the parish to make use of it, particularly the black fleeces.

MARGARET: The fuchsia's been jumping out at me all summer. The lovely blackberry. Autumn brings strong colours – the orange bracken, the weather changing fast. Clouds. I also find myself studying rock formations more closely, thinking about how I might weave them so they look as natural as the landscape.

I suppose much of our work is very visual. We are drawn back to the Irish and Celtic landscape and the archaeology we see around us.

MÁIRE: The markings on the stones are brought to life by stories handed down. My roots are intertwined in all of this and I have a strong sense of belonging. Some of it is very spiritual. Reflecting both the pagan and Christian beliefs, archaeology, St Colmcille, *An Turas*, the pilgrimage.

MARGARET: The landscape and archaeology in our work may offer more heritage overtones, rather than suggesting only religious attributes.

*Fiddlers*, Sandra Mockler, 24"x48", natural dyes and hand spun yarn. 'This tapestry was one of my first and one of the hardest. I found the stripes difficult to weave and felt pressure to get the faces to resemble the people. But I loved the challenge. This tapestry celebrates well-known musicians from our area. One of them, Con Cassidy, is no longer living. The other is James Byrne'. This tapestry hangs in a pub in Carrick.

Collection of Paddy McGinley

Photo: Margaret Cunningham

*Utah* (detail), Margaret Cunningham

Collection of Liam Ronayne

Photo: Margaret Cunningham

*Mount Errigal*, Angela Byrne, 24"x 40", natural dyes and handspun yarn. This tapestry is one of Angela's first.

Collection of Ann Ueltschi

Photo: Ann Ueltschi

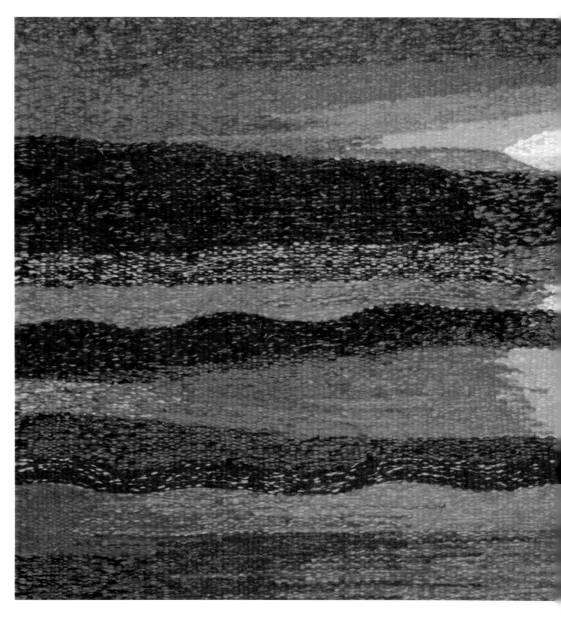

*Gath-Griene*, Golden Path of the Rays, Dermot Cannon, 30"x 30", commercial yarn.

'Sometimes I look at Dermot's tapestries and wonder where he saw all those vibrant colours. But then I'll be out driving past his house and see those colours perfectly'. – Margaret Cunningham

Collection of Joseph M. Murphy, Country Bank, Scarsdale, New York

Photo: Margaret Cunningham

It's more of our heritage and belief in St Colmcille.

MÁIRE: Religion is a big part of our heritage. In pre-Christian Ireland we had a very sophisticated religion known as the Celtic religion. Early missionaries such as St Colmcille used symbols and practices from the pre-Christian era and adapted them for their own spiritual use. Unlike other parts of Europe the transition here from paganism to Christianity was a peaceful one.

MARGARET: The thing I love about the archaeology is the fact that it has lasted for so long, you know. Someone thousands of years ago looked at these ruins too. You think, my God, and you wonder what they might have thought when they looked at it.

DERMOT: I don't know whether my work expresses a religious reaction to the landscape. A lot of it is just capturing a vision, texture, colour.

MARGARET: Sometimes I look at Dermot's tapestries and think, where did he see those vibrant colours? Then I'll be out, going here and there, driving past his house in the summer and turn around and see those colours perfectly. Some

of them a once-off glimpse. But they're there.

Our environment really does become one with the piece. Especially when we use local wool, local dyestuffs – the heather, lichens and all – the colour palette is lying out there in the beauty and life that we are surrounded by here.

## PERSONAL INFLUENCES

**Besides the environmental influences on your work such as landscape, archaeology and natural materials, were there any specific people or incidents that grew out of your lives in Glencolmcille, save for the mentors and others in local textile businesses whom I've interviewed for this project, who have made indelible artistic marks upon you?**

MARGARET: We had people in the family who were weavers. We've a background of it. But I hadn't really thought about it much until Monica de Bath came around recruiting for the cooperative. I remember thinking, gosh, I could learn these skills, they're part of me really. I felt proud of the fact my relatives wove.

MÁIRE: My grandfather and grand uncles wove tweed. I always thought of it as a kind of slave labour back then. When I began weaving I never realized just how really skilled they were. The likes of them will never be again.

MARGARET: Once, while I was in Dublin at an exhibition sponsored by designers, I saw a basket, the likes of which I recognized and I asked the woman, 'Where did you get that basket?' She told me she had bought it forty years ago in Ardara. My uncle wove baskets like that. Seeing the basket made me feel part of it – the whole weaving tradition. Here I was in Dublin, but I felt a sudden connection with home, Donegal, and how my tapestry fitted in.

MÁIRE: My mother was an excellent dressmaker. I grew up with threads. She knitted as well. I don't know specifically how these things work out with the weaving but they do. They certainly do.

*Dance of Crabs*, Margaret Cunningham, 31"x 43", handspun yarn. This tapestry was inspired by the dance, The Siege of Ennis. 'I was in my "crab phase" at the time. My father worked in the fish factory. This piece celebrates that. He taught us to have great respect for fish and for the sea'.

Collection of William Morgan

Photo: Margaret Cunningham

MARGARET: Sure your mother has suggested ways to finish a tapestry.

**Tidy the top and bottom selvages?**

MÁIRE: Aye. She's been a help with ways to hang the piece as well, I suppose.

DERMOT: There's plenty of people around with talent. We wouldn't have had any instruction in school, but there's plenty of musicians, dancers and painters.

MARGARET: Have you met Kenneth King? He's a local marine painter. He came in several times to our workshop. He's a grand fella! We were encouraged to visit him and see his work, which is very highly skilled. I was fascinated by him telling me if he feels like moving rocks in the painting to where he desires, that it was quite all right; it gave me encouragement to interpret landscapes in my own fashion.

MÁIRE: Him visiting us gave our own work validation.

MARGARET: Then there's the fact that the

musicians come to Glen. They remember and encourage you. And they like to come here for inspiration from our music and the craic. We benefit from that energy.

DERMOT: Sandra Mockler wove a tapestry, *Fiddlers,* about the local musicians Con Cassidy, who is no longer living, and James Byrne. It hangs in a pub in Carrick.

**Margaret, you play guitar and sing. Do you see any similarities between the music, dancing and weaving?**

MARGARET: I think people who enjoy one, appreciate the other. People who like the traditional songs really enjoy our tapestries connected with local lore. My tapestry, *Waves of Tory,* is based on the dance tune of the same name. *Dance of Crabs* is based on the dance, The Siege of Ennis.

**How do the crabs figure into these pieces?**

MARGARET: [laughs] I was in my 'crab phase' at the time. My father worked in the fish factory. I was celebrating that. Did you notice that between the crabs are chromosomes? Little Xs and Ys. They would be the dance partners.

DERMOT: [grinning] She keeps us amused.

## GLOBAL INFLUENCES

I spoke with Conal McIntyre [a former Taipéis Gael weaver] last night, and he was telling me about the time he spent living and working among the Bedouin people in the Middle East and Africa, and how this experience inspired him as an artist. He said, 'Some Bedouin lived in tents woven by women in rich browns and earthy tones that I found fascinating. They often used bright, primary colours in embroidered clothes and jewellery against backings of black, and the effect was stunning'.

All of you are clearly influenced by your surroundings, and I am aware that you've taken part in workshops with weavers from other countries. Is there a specific culture from

which you have learned or gained inspiration?

MÁIRE: I find myself practising techniques from other cultures more so than, say, their designs. I've a book on Native American rug patterns that I've used to practise shapes. I don't know that you could look at any one of my tapestries thus far and notice another culture's influence but their colours, patterns and knots may be in it.

In my Famine tapestry, *Cén Fáth*, I borrowed the shapes I saw in an image of a Native American or Canadian Chilkat blanket from the late 1800s. I wanted to incorporate a native design to recognize the contribution American Indians made to the people of Ireland at the time. It also raises the question, are less well-off communities across all cultures more generous and giving in times of need?

### Why the title *Cén Fáth*?

MÁIRE: It means 'Why?' and it invites people to question why, in a land of abundance, did people die of hunger?

MARGARET: Native American themes have appeared in my work as well. I consciously planned this in my Famine tapestries. I wanted to give recognition to the Native Americans who sent money to Ireland then, so I wove their symbols into more than one piece.

I've also explored the colours and rock-art images of the American Southwest. There are some similarities in the prehistoric art there to Ireland's. For example, the endless spirals we see carved into rocks here are also carved in the rock art of the American West. My tapestry *An Turas* incorporates the spiral and the yellows and pinks of the desert in a piece that was about St Colmcille's pilgrimage here.

And I often saw a wee man called Kokapelli, a fertility symbol in the American West. I associated him with Ireland's own Sheela na Gig and wove them together in one of these Famine tapestries – again, drawing on those connections.

**Dermot, you are working on a piece now with Turkish knots, the sort that makes a pile carpet. Will you do more with this?**

DERMOT: I felt like experimenting. It's a small piece; I didn't make a sketch, just wanted to see how it went. It feels good, the soft weft. It's a slow process, having to tie on and cut off each knot. I can appreciate the time that goes into Oriental carpets.

In some ways, this is the method I use to make a Ram tapestry. It's the same kind of knot, only I'm using a real lock of sheep's wool rather than a thread. No cutting is needed as I leave it the natural length of the fleece. And of course it works up faster because I'm using more fibre than a single-spun thread.

**The Ram design was one of Conal Gillespie's originals, wasn't it?**

DERMOT: Aye. People love them. Since Conal left, I carried on. We probably sell one a year.

**It is an ingenious idea. With real rams' horns as well. How do you get them to attach to the tapestry?**

DERMOT: Ah, they're tied on, just like the threads. Drill a couple holes into the horn and tie it on.

**Any other ideas that arose from what artists do elsewhere?**

MÁIRE: I was impressed with the Spanish–American weavers at Tierra Wools in New Mexico. Especially the set up of their cooperative – with sheep, dye gardens and a showroom all together. Visitors get an immediate sense of what goes into their weaving.

And the Americans we met at workshops and conferences. Everyone has something to offer. Everyone was welcoming of us on our Southwest tour, interested in what we were weaving. They motivated us to keep at it. Many of them are exploring natural dyes with great success. It's an incentive for us to keep it up here, and also to try a few dyestuffs that aren't indigenous to Ireland.

These people also inspired me to grow my own dye garden. Actually one of the reasons we moved from our original studio was so

*Screag Beefan*, Rocky Crag at Beefan, Margaret Cunningham, 27"x 44", commercial and handspun yarn. This tapestry, which shows the Beefan portion of Glen Head, captures the colours of autumn. 'I hadn't wove such a close-up of rocks before. It involved a lot of blending of natural, homespun colours. A woman from Kansas bought it before I had even cut it down from the loom'.

Collection Of Gordon and Suzanne Kingsley

Photo: Margaret Cunningham

*Teach Solais*, Lighthouse, Dermot Cannon, 29"x 42", natural dyes and handspun yarn. The four eyes in the foreground of the tapestry represent the lighthouse keepers who manned the light for years. The fish and seal represent those who reaped from these rich waters under harsh conditions.

'I wove this during the two-year training course. I used very thick handspun, sometimes using four strands at a time. I think that's what gave this piece its vibrancy. The vertical lines were very difficult and required many joins. This tapestry was the first I sold'.

Collection of Ann Ueltschi

Photo: Margaret Cunningham

we could do more with the natural dyes. We weren't set up for it in Oideas Gael.

**Is natural dyeing part of the workshops you offer here in Malinbeg?**

MÁIRE: We've demonstrated it for students in the past. But right now it's not our focus, as we're just getting settled here. But it's not to say it couldn't be.

## ADVANTAGE OF HOMESPUN

**When I come here, I often see Dermot spinning. Do you all spin your own yarns? How does this affect production?**

MARGARET: I use a bit of homespun in all my tapestries. But I like the sharp edges I get with the commercially spun yarns. It takes an enormous amount of time to spin wool. We often can't work with it as much as we'd like.

MÁIRE: Going back to the traditional methods of preparing my materials is important to me because it keeps me in tune with nature from start to finish.

MARGARET: It's very welcoming to me to use the natural, undyed black, grey and white wool of the sheep to fulfill the texture of rocks.

DERMOT: [smiling at Margaret] I knew a lot of my homespun had gone missing.

MARGARET: [laughs] One of my favourite local landscapes that I'm most pleased with is *Scrig Beefan* (named after a place on Glen Head). I hadn't done such a close-up of rocks before. It involved a lot of blending of homespun colours. I remember a woman from Kansas bought it before I'd even cut it from the loom.

**Why do you weave with it, Dermot?**

DERMOT: I enjoy the process really. The carding

Máire paints
watercolours for
commissions before
weaving a design.

and spinning. I like the feel of it. A Cheviot wool is softer than the commercial yarn we use. Sometimes I mix the two together for different textures in a piece.

**Does this cause any problems structurally, such as with the tension?**

DERMOT: I've woven some tapestries with edges that weren't so straight. But after a while you look out for that. Try to compensate as you go. My first lighthouse tapestry consisted of four homespun strands woven together. It was a very thick tapestry! I thought I'd get it finished faster by using four threads. I didn't anticipate the movement of the warp from packing in all that weft. But I was stuck with the four strands until the end.

**It looks like you succeeded. Anything unexpected come of it?**

DERMOT: Aye, I was pleased with it in the end. But I stayed away from it the next time. There were lots of vertical lines in the lighthouse. Many joins. 'Twas slow. But I believe it was the four strands together that gave the piece its vibrancy, three dimensionality, and its movement of colour and line. Not that I'd known at the time to plan for – it was my first piece ever.

**Máire, your work is rich in texture too. What is your experience with commercial versus homespun yarn?**

MÁIRE: One thing I learned early is that homespun – the slubby kind beginners tend to make – is very hard to weave into geometric figures. One of my first tapestries, *An Aonach* (Stone of the Fair), was designed after an image on a standing stone in Glencolmcille. It involved circles and measuring. No freedom in it as you wove. The inconsistent widths of the yarn proved it is nearly impossible to pull off a circle. It's funny though, now that I'm a better spinner, I can't make the thick, slubby yarn anymore. It's harder to get that effect for other projects when you want it.

**Margaret, I've seen you weave with sewing thread. How has that worked for you?**

MARGARET: I've used all kinds of fibres in my tapestries in combination with different types of knots for texture. In some cases the thin sewing threads or silk will highlight places. I find that by spinning different threads together, I can create new colours and textures. Sometimes two threads of the same shade, but different textures, give a pleasing effect.

The knots make different patterns on the background. I've used a technique of weaving in triangle shapes that not only adds interest and dimension but helps with the elasticity of the piece and with attaining straight edges such as in *An Turas*. Vertical soumak knots – wrapping weft around pairs of warp – are good for tackling joins and accentuating vertical lines, as in *Belief in Colmcille*.

**Would anyone care to describe the looms you use? What other equipment, if any, is needed to weave tapestry?**

DERMOT: We've always woven on simple picture-frame looms, the size depending on the tapestry. A local carpenter puts them together for us. They're inexpensive.

MARGARET: We work on upright looms. Warp threads are attached individually at the top and bottom of the frame. I like working with this design because I feel the frame is strong and I feel I can make a rigid piece on it with good edges.

The design is woven from the front by passing weft thread, back and forth in most cases, between each vertical warp. There's nothing mechanical about it. It's all done by finger-picking.

Another advantage of this type of a loom, as opposed to one with rolling beams for the top or bottom frame, is that you see the whole tapestry as you work your way from the bottom to top. The bottom of the tapestry can't be rolled under and around the beam out of sight, a feature that fancier looms offer – enabling the weaver to make a piece larger than the space within the frame.

## ART AND SPONTANEITY

MÁIRE: Other equipment we use include xerox machines and over head projectors. For large tapestries, I've sketched designs, projected them on to the wall and traced the enlarged image onto poster paper.

**Are there any other techniques you might suggest? What about the use of photographs and cartoons?**

DERMOT: I like to work off photographs every so often. Use them for a base line and improvise.

MARGARET: I have to admit I am a great user of photography in my work. I prefer to use only my own photographs. I might take several pictures of a landscape at different times of the day to capture the light, shading. Find one that matches what I have in mind. The colours I weave into the piece as well as the shapes that emerge, usually enhance the original photo interpretation.

MÁIRE: I've used photographs. Sometimes they help when you are making a local landscape, so you get the lie of the land right, so you are not working from memory.

**I've heard different opinions about whether painters or artists should use photographs in their work. Some suggest it is copying some other original work and therefore the result of using a photograph could only be considered unoriginal and therefore not art. What have you to say in response to this?**

MÁIRE: I agree with Margaret that the weaving or interpretation of a photograph pushes the use of it toward art. I don't think any artist would enjoy replicating what someone else has already done. It's a very hard task for a tapestry weaver to replicate a photograph anyway. We are limited by the colours of our thread, the geometric nature of a warp and weft. A painter

has more freedom to blend colours and swish the brush in shapes that are difficult to achieve through weaving.

**How about cartoons? Is there anything to be gained or lost in their use?**

DERMOT: I've worked with and without them. I did weave a few cottages and landscapes that were totally made up and wove them without a cartoon. I saw this at the time as an evolution in my skills. It was a bit scary at first. A challenge to face a blank warp with no cartoon behind it.

Other times I've kept a photograph beside me and worked from it with no cartoon actually beside the loom. With these I played with the colours.

**What about your sunset tapestries? Are these from cartoons?**

DERMOT: No. They are just what I see. I like to capture the fine gradation of colour in the sun's reflection off water. For these I've been using commercially spun yarn to get the sharp edge Margaret has talked about. The uniform thread makes finer transitions and joins. My more recent sunsets are in greys and blues. Something different. I like the mood of them. I've woven off Máire's sketches, as well. *Colmcille in Exile* is a version of Máire's cartoon.

MÁIRE: In doing this it is amazing how Dermot retained his own signature on the piece. Again, I think this speaks to what we just said about copying a photograph. Dermot wouldn't have woven in all the detail on the original sketch. I like his interpretation of it. It's fresh with clear and simple lines.

MARGARET: I always prefer to use a cartoon for tapestries. They give me a sense of direction. And if you are weaving a commission, the customer usually wants to see the whole story at the beginning. Businesses, in particular, often have to sell the concept or image to the person who will pay for it.

*An Ghorta*, The Famine, Dermot Cannon, detail.

See full image on page 122.

**So that spontaneous creative rush comes in the sketch rather than at the loom?**

Máire: Well, the design part can sometimes be very hard, like work. Particularly if it is a commission. You can spend weeks with designers. If it's a piece I design entirely for myself, with no buyer in mind, both the sketch and the weaving of it can feel creative all the way through.

The creation of your own colours, through the blending of existing yarns or spinning and dyeing of your own. The way you weave the scene – knots, patterns incorporated. So knowing the end, the 'big picture', wouldn't really detract from the creative pleasure of the process.

Dermot: In my *Famine* tapestry . . .

**Now my Famine tapestry?**

Dermot: The very one. I started with a sketch. I made up the design based on things I had read about the Famine: the potato blight, coffin ships and the like. But the dead man just happened.

So did the clouds, which mirrored and in a sense shadowed the geese. So I think there is always room for surprise and there will be surprise in nearly every piece, cartoon or not.

Margaret: And I think it's those elements that people respond to.

**Though I had personal reasons for buying this particular tapestry, I have to say it was the dead man that convinced me this tapestry was for me.**

## Weaving Challenges

**Is there anything in particular you find difficult to weave? For example, when I spoke with Sandra Mockler [a former Taipéis Gael weaver] yesterday, she said that weaving faces challenge her. Though this hasn't kept her from working on a tapestry based on a wedding photograph of her parents.**

Dermot: [immediately] Letters. I ripped out many of them on the fishing ships I wove. The ships themselves are hard to do. Lots of detail.

*Split Tree*, Margaret Cunningham, detail, commercial yarn. Detail of a tapestry based on the poem, *St Patrick and the Four Masters* by Charles Beamer, a writer from Texas (see p.130). 'This is the first time I designed a tapestry based on someone else's work. I think it's good to get out of our own spheres; things open up'.

Collection of Charles and Alice Beamer

Photo: Mark Butler

But the letters I found the hardest.

MÁIRE: I find it hard to show the sheer steepness in the cliffs here. Sometimes it comes across with a good sketch, sometimes not.

MARGARET: I think vertical lines are always a challenge because they demand so many joins. Like I've said, I've used soumak knots at times for this. I've also used a pointed dovetail knot which I learned in Denmark. This method weaves up quickly. Or weaving a tapestry sideways so that the vertical lines are horizontal while weaving.

Another would be a commission I wove from Máire's design, *Ag Seoltoireacht* (Sailing). This one needed to be followed closely. Since I hadn't drawn it, for some reason it posed more of a challenge. At the same time I really enjoyed it.

MÁIRE: I find small pieces harder to weave. I can't get a story into them. For a while we were weaving smaller pieces that we could bring overseas to workshops, or to keep here for tourists who might take one home in their suitcase. I found that I mostly experimented with shapes, or practised images from weaving books on the smaller pieces.

## ART AND FOLK ART

The folklorist Henry Glassie said that fine art is the product of secular societies and folk art is the product of religious societies. Folk art has a tendency to withdraw from the world toward the spiritual. Folk artists are not anachronistic. They are driven by the past and their tradition directs them clearly toward life to come.

Conal McIntyre responded to this by saying that he doesn't agree with Henry Glassie at all. He said, 'Some of the world's best-known artists had deep religious convictions – William Blake, Van Gogh, the Italian masters,

etc. Folk art often focuses on the ritual, myths, the exterior imagery of religion rather than the spiritual journey of the soul. I do not see my work as folk art'.

**How do you respond to this?**

MÁIRE: Until this question was posed, I never thought about putting a label on my work, such as 'fine art' or 'folk art'. I think the term 'folk art' would suit best because my work would largely reflect the traditional culture in my area. The art content in my pieces comes from my own raw intuition rather than from any standard of formal art training.

**In what ways might your work, as Glassie says, 'do the work of philosophy, open minds to enduring problems for contemplation?' For example, Conal McIntyre responded to this question on an abstract level.** He said, 'The spirit of man comes through our language and art. So whether we are wrestling in the dark or celebrating the light, something of that inner light spills out, especially in creative expressions'.
 A more tangible example, I think, may be Conal McIntyre's tapestry *Convergence*, his piece that addresses issues between the old Republican and Unionists tribes in Northern Ireland. About this he said, 'It's an issue of polarization I can never disassociate myself from even though so many others do. This work illustrates a trail of history left behind by the two cultures, signified by flags and blocks – black and white thinking – yet hope, in the form of

*Convergence*, Conal McIntyre, size 24"x48", commercial yarn. This tapestry addresses the Troubles between the old Republican and Unionists tribes in Northern Ireland. 'It's an issue of polarization I can never dissociate myself from even when so many others do. This work illustrates a trail of history left behind by two cultures, signified by flags and blocks – black and white thinking. Yet hope, in the form of a dove, hovers over it all. I think we Irish need to tell our stories, history, lore and the lot, but we've got to be conscious of the world we live in. Try to bring the two sides together, if only in a piece of tapestry'.

Collection of Barclays Bank, Dublin

Photo: Conal McIntyre

Máire at work on a
design.

a dove, hovers over it all. I think we Irish need to tell our stories, history, lore and the lot, but we've got to be conscious of the world we live in. Try to bring the two sides together if only in a piece of tapestry'.

MÁIRE: I think some of our earlier work with Danish artists and Irish Travellers, such as *Cultural Symbols,* which addresses voices from 'the margins', speaks to this notion. And I guess my Famine tapestry, *Cén Fáth,* which I mentioned earlier, throws out for contemplation the question, how in a land of abundance could the Irish have died of starvation? And who tends to help the suffering – 'the haves' or the 'have nots'?

MARGARET: In a way our cooperative embodies this idea. Artists from the Gaeltacht have a voice, too, among the arts community in Ireland, and the world, even. It's about inclusion, representation, acknowledgment and legitimacy.

Lately, I've been weaving poems. It's been a way of connecting with other artists' inner light. I've quite enjoyed it. The first tapestry I wove to this end was *Bonnán Buí* (Yellow Bittern). It is a poem I had memorized for the Leaving Certificate from secondary school. I wasn't concerned at all about whether it would sell.

The next one I tried was a poem written by a writer from Texas, Charles Beamer, whom I mentioned before. I connected with one stanza in particular from his poem, 'St Patrick and the Four Masters:'

> *Perhaps the trees spoke first*
> *during the migrations, the sunderings;*
> *perhaps the first dialogues*
> *about the web and spirit between earth and sky*

This notion of trees speaking first. I immediately saw the tree in my grandmother's yard, the one we often gathered around for family photographs. It had just been split by storms that week – a direct dialogue between earth and sky. And so I went from there.

This was the first time I wove something based on someone else's work. I had to get into his place, his spirit, so to speak. I remember I sat and read his poem because I couldn't get into my work on the loom at the time due to a storm. And images began to come to me. I think it's good to get out of our own spheres; things open up.

## Art or Craft

**Is there any question in your minds whether or not tapestry in general, and your work in particular, falls into the category of art or craft? What do you make of these categories? How does this affect your art or business, if at all?**

Máire: This issue comes up often, as we are a business of artists. If you are making a living of your art, you are in some ways treating it like a craft because of the selling, the pricing. You nearly have to standardize the price by square foot with tapestry. No one would put a price on a painting in this way. Customers lose sight of the time that might go into a design. Sometimes you spend weeks, but they don't see it. They sometimes understand that a handspun piece should be worth more than a commercial yarn piece. So in the end, it's the size of tapestry that often determines the price. Even if a wee tapestry actually took longer from start to finish!

Margaret: Our work is original and therefore would be considered art rather than craft. There's no kind of rigid control involved to get each piece similar as you would likely see in craft.

**Such as the way the old sweater-knitting cooperatives organized by Gaeltarra Éireann worked years ago?**

Margaret: Aye. Even if we were to make a replica of a tapestry for someone who liked one we'd already sold, no two tapestries would be alike. Each of us interprets a theme in our own way. None of us would feel a creative spark by repeating exactly something we've done before. The spark is what keeps us weaving.

**Conal McIntyre responded to this same question in his home last night. He said, 'If the weaver has created the design, that is art. A craft would be where someone presents you with an image and you execute it. Like giving a suit to a tailor'. Do you agree or disagree with these thoughts?**

Margaret: Aye. The design part would be art. In some ways tapestry is half art, half craft. You learn the skills with which to execute the design. You may even make your own thread, which could be both art and craft. It is art if you're designing your own thread. The tweed weavers of old would have aimed for specifically spun threads for warp and weft, not deviating from those parameters. But as tapestry artists, we would look toward departing from those limitations.

**What about the use of photographs?**

Dermot: I think if you put your own interpretation on that photograph it pushes it toward art. And if it's your photograph to begin with, then the perspective with which you've taken it is certainly original.

**Another idea Conal raised is the notion that an artist is moved by something enough – be it colour, shape, or commentary on life – and will create something from there. An artist's goal isn't necessarily to sell it. If people like it in the end, all the better.**

Máire: The business of what to make is a part of what it means to be an arts cooperative. A commissioned piece can be both art and craft for the weaver, depending on the amount of design that comes from the artist.

Margaret at work.

**So you would agree with Conal that design is a key element that distinguishes an artist from a craftsperson?**

DERMOT: An artist is a craftsperson, but not vice versa.

MÁIRE: But I am not sure how this would apply to a painter. Unless the painter made his own paints, then that could be considered craft.

MARGARET: The skills and techniques of painting or weaving could be considered craft. It's where we push those skills that is art.

**Conal touched on this as well. He said, 'Tapestry in and of itself is not necessarily art or craft; it is a medium like anything else, such as paint, wood or stone. As tapestry artists we have the responsibility to experiment and develop our skills with the medium'. Would you interpret this as meaning that education enters into**

**what it means to be an artist?**

MARGARET: To some extent. I know I benefited from art instruction. But I haven't learned my ideas or inspirations from a book.

MÁIRE: I think to be considered an artist you have to be satisfying yourself in some way. You must be working on the piece because you want to. It's different than I imagine working on a craft, producing something again and again.

**I think Conal would agree. He said, 'I am interested in learning the basic techniques and will then go on to experiment. I would rather do something riddled with mistakes, yet full of life, than something highly polished'.**

MÁIRE: Aye. And I think that's where art departs from craft.

**We touched briefly on this notion that artists have a responsibility to push their skills. What**

have you done in this respect or what direction are you heading?

DERMOT: I might try some bigger, more abstract landscapes. Maybe experiment some more with Turkish knots – the pile rug type.

MARGARET: I'd like to weave something for myself! Something purely experimental that I have no worries in the back of my mind as to whether it will sell. I'm working on a piece at home based on one of my paintings that I'd like to get into a juried exhibition.

I also want to go big! Like those old Danish tapestries. I'd like to use other materials such as linen and cloth.

And I'd like to go on a retreat of some kind and read up on a few things in the arts that I'm interested in; play around with design; and even do a bit of writing or songwriting.

MÁIRE: I like working with human figures. I'd like to push my skills in this area. I'd also like to become more abstract. Try to create something that you can keep discerning every time you look at it. See something new, hidden.

## COMMUNITY ROLE-MODELS

How much of a role does teaching play in your work at Taipéis Gael? And how does that add to or take away from your own weaving?

MARGARET: We teach most of the summer. We always learn something from the students. They come with fresh ideas. In many cases these people are artists of some kind, and we benefit from their expertise and perspective. We had an art teacher visit once who always had her ear to the ground for courses. She's passed this information on to us and has also told others about us.

MÁIRE: Aye. They genuinely want to be part of it, help you, give their opinions. It's a wonderful way to make contacts. Some even lead to sales or commissions or invitations to teach elsewhere.

*Cultural Symbols*, 10'x 1', commercial yarn. This tapestry arose from a workshop in 1994 sponsored by the Task Force of the European Union Arts, Education and Training Initiative. One of the goals of the Initiative is to engage in activities that enhance cross-cultural progress above economic development in a way that respects the identities of peripheral and marginalized communities.

Three cultures came together with Taipéis Gael to weave this tapestry under the direction of Theresa McKenna, National College of Art and Design: Danish, Irish Travellers and Thai refugees living in Denmark. A workshop in Dublin allowed these communities of weavers to tell their stories in a new way. Most of the symbols express the human need to travel, both physically and spiritually: wheels represent transport and the Irish Traveller lifestyle; the boulders depict the obstacles and prejudices that are often in the Travellers' path; a Thai goddess is seen as a spiritual link for a Thai immigrant to her homeland as she forges a new life in Denmark; the cow is representative of a once-rural way of life, common to all cultures; and the outstretched hands are symbols of human struggle and of reaching out to others to withstand inhumanity.

Taipéis Gael Weavers: Conal Gillespie, Margaret Cunningham and Monica de Bath

Danish Weavers: Britta Bertelsen and Lisa Bisbelle

Thai weaver: Vilai

Irish Travellers: Bernadette Collins and Julie Joyce

DERMOT: We normally weave along with the students, so it doesn't really take away from the time we need for our own work.

MARGARET: After a day or two when the students have learned the basic techniques, they get so enthusiastic they don't stop for lunch or take any breaks. It's a great atmosphere for me to work in.

**What other hats must you wear as a member of a cooperative, beside weaver and teacher?**

DERMOT: Public speaking. Setting up exhibitions. Sales and commissions. We all do a bit of this.

MÁIRE: Annie has worked with us on making a business plan. But it seems we keep changing it all the time!

MARGARET: I think partly we need to respond to opportunities as they arise. We can't foresee when someone will land a big commission for us that might involve all of us weaving to meet that deadline, or when an exhibition arises, etc. There's always a certain amount of shuffling involved.

As a group, we have an advantage. We can cover all bases if need be, whereas a single artist would have a hard time. We can even be in two places at once!

Our flexibility helps too. The others are encouraging when I go off with the band for a tour. They know that I promote Taipéis Gael wherever I go.

MÁIRE: I often think it's a miracle. But we've worked hard to stay together. I think it's the camaraderie we share that keeps us going. And the fact that we have Annie. Not many artists have the luxury of a business manager. She fills a tremendous role and need.

**What plans do you have for the future?**

MARGARET: I would like to work on a very large piece, and also explore with other mediums such as felt, incorporating it into tapestry.

I see us looking into joint exhibitions with other weavers outside of Taipéis Gael, or mixed media shows with other local artists. I wouldn't mind doing a solo exhibition of my own work. What we've learned over the past ten years and our experiences as a group have set us up for going in any number of directions.

MÁIRE: I'd like to make a dye garden and increase the amount of homepsun and naturally dyed yarns we use in our work, organize the studio and the outside environment so it explains better the process of weaving a tapestry from the fleece.

DERMOT: Just keep on the same path. Increase our sales if we can. Exhibitions.

**Conal McIntyre, when asked what one of his most memorable moments in tapestry said, 'When the design comes together'. Sandra Mockler said, 'Cutting a tapestry from the loom and having a look at it'. Would any of you like to share your most memorable moment?**

MARGARET: I'd have to say they would have occurred at one of our larger exhibitions in New York or Dublin where large crowds turned out. And also when you sell a piece. But some of those sweet moments are to be contrasted with moments when you feel like, 'Oh No!' when you've sold a piece that you really like and are sorry that you didn't buy it yourself. I feel that way about one tapestry.

DERMOT: I'd have to agree with Sandra. My most memorable moment was when after weaving for three months on my first tapestry, *Lighthouse*, when I cut it off the loom.

**Lastly, part of your mission statement as a cooperative is 'Weaving a Future from Our Past'. In light of this and your former residence in Oideas Gael, I wonder if you initially felt obliged to weave heritage pieces, and if you ever felt 'on stage' as a result of giving classes or lectures to the students there? Did you ever feel anachronistic or as if you were re-enacting the past. Do you ever feel this way now?**

Dermot at work.

MÁIRE: During our training we were encouraged to work to a theme. Because of the richness of our cultural heritage, there was no shortage for stories – archaeology, folklore, social history, etc. But in a way, passing on the traditional skills feels a bit like re-enacting the past.

MARGARET: It made sense for us to look to our natural resources and heritage at first to give us a sense of belonging to our design. Creating from our own culture. However, commissions sometimes depart from these themes; we do not always get to choose the subject matter, so we may or may not be weaving our past. Now, I think I subconsciously link back to my heritage as themes for tapestries I weave for exhibitions.

I am always on stage as an artist, ready to articulate the essence of the tapestry to the onlooker. Working in a cultural centre was enormous encouragement because there was always an appreciative eye passing through to view the work. I never felt, and don't feel now, as if I am re-enacting the past because I look at my subject with my own eyes, twenty-first century eyes. The skill of weaving may be a re-enactment in itself, but it is what one chooses to do with that skill that is the key – the creation of the new, carrying the art into the future.

# Gallery of Tapestries

# St Colmcille

*Dove of the Church*, Máire McGinley, 30"x48", natural dyes and handspun yarn. The Latin name for Colm is *Columba*, dove. Colm Cille means 'Dove of the Church'. This tapestry draws on the early Christian period to illustrate the significant events in the life of St Colmcille. Many of the symbols are taken from the standing stones, which make up *An Turas*, the saint's pilgrimage in Glencolmcille.

'Colmcille is represented by the bird in this piece. A crown signifies his noble lineage. The staff indicates his religious life of prayer, study and physical hardship. The cooking pot and fish typify the requirement of self-sufficiency in monastic life – testimony to the saint's life on Iona.

An integral part of the Columban monastic tradition was that of manuscript illumination and transcription, depicted by the book in this tapestry. Other works in this tradition are the Books of Durrow, Lindisfarne, Kells and the *Cathach*, the last of which is popularly ascribed to the Saint himself.

The tapestry also conveys the folklore of early Christian Ireland. The moon and sun is the passing of time, and the eye is the pagan practice of predicting the future – rituals addressed by Colmcille'.
Collection of Credit Union, Gweedore, County Donegal

Photo: Máire McGinley

*In Celebration of Colmcille*, Máire McGinley, 36"x43", commercial yarn. This piece was commissioned by Letterkenny Institute of Technology for their oratory. The dove represents the Holy Spirit coming to give the students inspiration through St Colmcille, who is known as the 'Dove of the Church'.

Collection of Letterkenny Institute of Technology

Photo: Máire McGinley

*On Wing and Wave*,
Conal McIntyre, 23"x
42", commercial yarn.
This tapestry is about
the spiritual inspiration
of Colmcille's life,
one based on the
scriptures, suggested
by the pages of the
open Bible at the base
of this piece. A Celtic
cross in the centre is a
symbol of Christianity.
Woven into the wave
is Columba and his
followers on their
way to Iona. The large
wave represents the
wave of Christian
revival, stemming
from Colmcille, which
spread across Europe
in the sixth century.
'The dove is the spirit
of God, without whom
Colmcille's message
would remain only
words'.

Collection of Liam Ó
Cuinneagáin

Photo: Conal McIntyre

*Sciochan t Cuimhlint*, Calming of the Waters, Máire McGinley, 26"x 49", commercial yarn. This tapestry explores the mixed emotions Colmcille felt about his exile to Iona following the conflict over the *Book of Gospels*, which he had copied to help spread the word to all believers, but was found guilty of copyright infringement. His verdict, 'to every cow its calf and to every book its copy'.

'The dove at the top is himself. Bloodied waters represent the battle over the book. But as time passed, the water ran clear and Colmcille is remembered as the great evangelist down through the centuries by all denominations'.

Collection Of Liam Ó Cuinneagáin

Photo: Máire McGinley

*Stásiún Cholmcille*, St Colmcille Station, Margaret Cunningham, 24"x30", natural dyes and handspun yarn. One of Margaret's early tapestries celebrating the local tradition, *An Turas*.

'This tapestry explores Turkish kilim weaving and a plain weave. I wove it in a course that explored different weavings from around the world'.

Collection of Tate Donovan

Photo: Margaret Cunningham

*Belief in Colmcille*, Margaret Cunningham, 40"x 40", commercial yarn. 'This tapestry celebrates pride in this saint, who is closely associated with the parish of Glencolmcille. To the right of the tapestry is the robed figure of Colmcille in a boat. On his right is one of the symbols of the station at the holy well in Beefan. To the left are silhouettes of people travelling the station at midnight, which is a more difficult time to do it. At the top are two people representing the older generation, who have helped keep the tradition alive in Glencolmcille'.

Collection of Joseph M. Murphy, Country Bank, Scarsdale, New York

Photo: Margaret Cunningham

*Siombailí Colmcille*,
Colmcille Symbols,
Margaret Cunningham,
32"x46", commercial
yarns. This tapestry
is dedicated to the
1400th anniversary
of St Colmcille. The
background is derived
from a photograph of a
section of rock. 'Rock
is fundamental to the
story of Colmcille'.
This image, in a sense,
is an aerial view of the
pilgrimage route, *An
Turas Cholmcille'*.

Walking this route
as a child, Margaret
recalls St Colmcille's
Boat – fashioned of
stones – and the reeds
that cut into her tiny
untoughened feet.
The symbols she has
woven into this piece
include a Christianized
pillar stone (now
a station of the
pilgrimage), and a hint
of a book (top left),
which is linked to the
legacy of this saint's
copyright scandal
after Colmcille's exile
to Iona following the
conflict over the *Book
of Gospels* (which he
had copied to help
spread the word to
all believers), but
was found guilty of
copyright infringement.
His verdict was 'to
every cow its calf and
to every book its copy'.

Collection of Charles
and Alice Beamer

Photo: Mark Butler

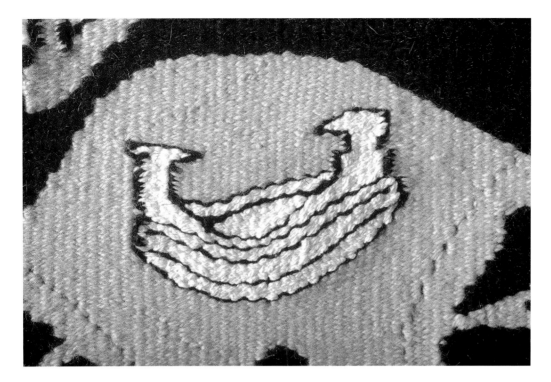

Detail from *Siombailí Colmcille*, Colmcille Symbols, Margaret Cunningham. St Colmcille's Boat. Between stations eight and nine of *An Turas Cholmcille* is a large rock – shaped like a boat – that contains a water hole where pilgrims wash their feet.

Collection of Charles and Alice Beamer

Photo: Mark Butler

*Cloch An Aonach*, Stone of the Gatherings, Máire McGinley, 24"x 36", natural dyes and handspun yarns. This image comes from a holed pillar stone, Station Nine of *An Turas*, the local pilgrimage. Tradition calls for couples becoming engaged to entwine their fingers through the hole, performing the ceremony in front of witnesses. Pilgrims who peer through while in the state of grace will receive a glimpse of heaven.

'Weaving this tapestry wasn't easy. There is a lot of measuring involved in making circles; you don't have the freedom of crafting as you go. The handspun yarn for this piece came out of my early spinning and was uneven in thickness, which also proved difficult for clean geometric figures. But it gave a nice texture, something I try to repeat now and again, but can't, because lately I'm spinning more finely'.

Collection of Eileen Moore Quinn

Photo: Eileen Moore Quinn

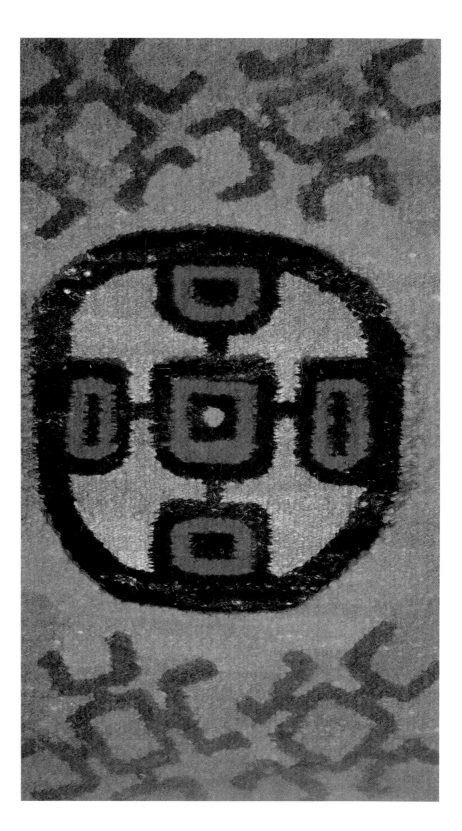

*Stásiún Colmcille*,
St Colmcille Station,
Conal McIntyre,
23"x42", commercial
yarn. Woven in
commemoration of
the saint's 1400th
birthday. 'This is one
piece in a series of
standing stones. Here
the movement in
the flowing bands of
colour are perhaps
enhanced by the
stillness of the stone'.

Collection of Joseph
M. Murphy, Country
Bank, Scarsdale,
New York

Photo: Conal McIntyre

*Strath na Circe,* Cerc's Swath, Margaret Cunningham, 24"x 36", commercial yarns. This tapestry is based on the story of Colmcille and the Demons.

'Legend holds that when Padraic banished the demons from Mayo, they went north and settled near Glencolmcille until the time of Colmcille. The demons raised a fog about them so that none could see the land that lay beneath. This fog is depicted by the grey border in this tapestry. The red in the background signifies the fiery stream that the demons raised, which no one could cross alive. Angels of God revealed the fiery stream to Colmcille, who went there with others to banish the demons. But when they arrived, the devil hurled a holly rod, which killed Cerc, Colmcille's servant. In anger, Colmcille took the rod and threw it across the stream and the demons fled to the sea, which is represented by the fish in the tapestry. A holly bush has forever remained unwithered at Strath na Circe with berries as red as the fiery stream'.

Collection of Joseph M. Murphy, Country Bank, Scarsdale, New York

Photo: Margaret Cunningham

*Litir*, The Letter, Monica de Bath, 30" x 42", handspun with natural dyes. For centuries letters have kept emigrants in touch with their homelands. Both Colmcille and Sheela na Gig (Celtic fertility goddess) were exiled. Colmcille sailed to Iona, and Sheela – in the form of stone carvings – was locked away in the vaults of museums. In this tapestry, Sheela na Gig writes to Colmcille, telling him of the freedom of flying calves, birds and fishes – all symbols from the *Book of Kells*.

Collection of Larry Fulhom

Photo: Monica de Bath

# The Famine

*An Ghorta Mór*, The Great Hunger, by Conal Gillespie, 48"x 30", natural dyes and handspun yarn. This piece shows people leaving the area or walking toward the sea in search of what sustenance they might reap there: dulce (seaweed), bird eggs from the cliffs, shellfish.

Collection of Ann Ueleschi

Photo: Ann Ueleschi

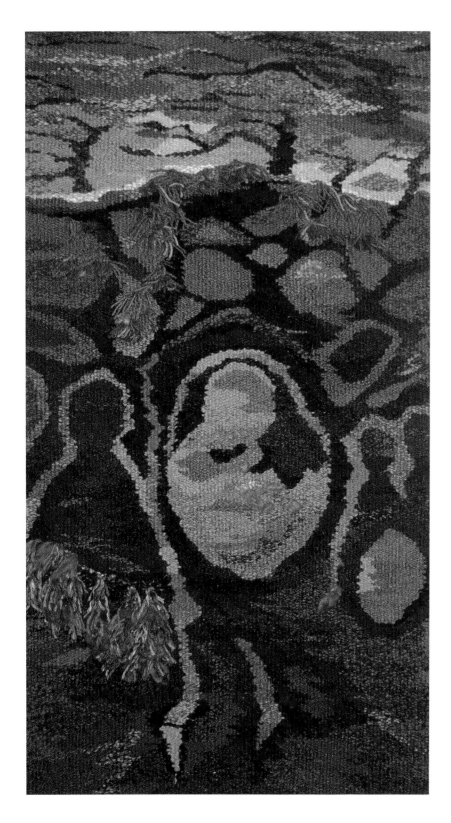

*An Ghorta Mór*, The Great Hunger, Conal McIntyre, 43"x 24", commercial yarn. A perspective on the Famine from beneath the turf.

Collection of Joseph M. Murphy, Country Bank, Scarsdale, New York

Photo: Conal McIntyre

*Balla An Ghorta*
Famine Wall I,
Margaret Cunningham,
size 30"x48",
commercial yarn. 'The
blue strokes in the
background depict the
stone walls that were
built during the Board
of Works scheme
introduced in the time
of the Famine. The F in
the centre is made up
of stripes from Famine
publications and
includes key words.
The red and yellow
throughout the piece
represent lives lost
and homes burned.
The grey-blue signifies
the blight creeping in,
which destroyed the
potato crop.

'American Indians
extended their help
to the Irish during
the Famine and this
is symbolized by the
hands and a whale
from their culture'.

Collection of Joseph
M. Murphy, Country
Bank, Scarsdale,
New York

Photo: Joe Vericker/
Photo Bureau

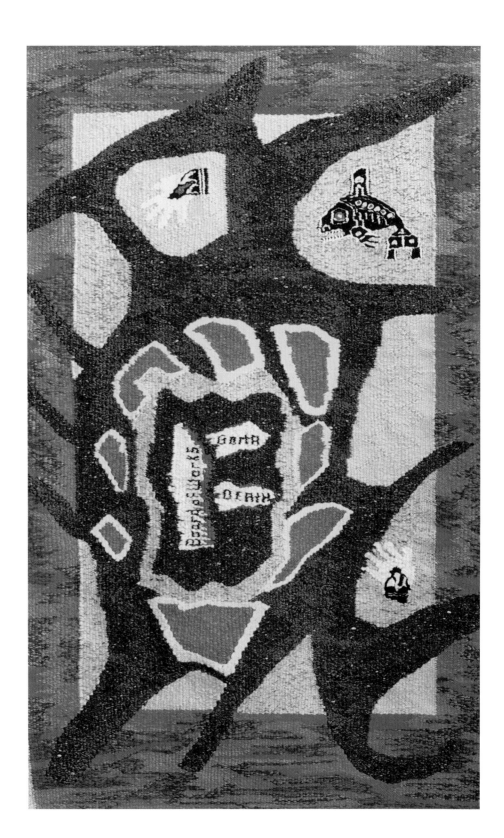

*Balla An Ghorta II*, Famine Wall II, Margaret Cunningham, 30"x 48", commercial yarn. 'While gathering images for my famine series, I came across a photograph of a house deserted during the Famine. The roof was gone, the windows broken, and walls were covered with green lichen. Out of this emerged the colour and shattered glass imagery for the background of this tapestry.

'On the lower right I have woven implements for gathering potatoes, and above this, a famine pot to feed the hungry.

'In my research, I discovered that American Indians helped the Irish by sending grain. To acknowledge this assistance, I chose fertility symbols of both cultures, Sheela na Gig (Celtic) and Kokapelli (Native American).

'They encircle the Glencolmcille Angel, a symbol of our parish. The angel represents the faith that carried our people through these hardships'.

Collection of Joseph M. Murphy, Country Bank, Scarsdale, New York

Photo: Joe Vericker/ Photo Bureau

*An Ghorta*, The Famine, Dermot Cannon, 48"x 30", natural dyes and handspun yarn. 'This tapestry is based on things I've read about the Great Hunger. The coffin ships, famine houses, or vacant homes, and such. Though I worked from a cartoon, the clouds mirroring the geese and the dead man just happened – there's room for surprise in any piece'.

Collection of Meghan and Bill Sayres

Photo: ChromoStat Photography, Spokane, Washington

# Literature, Legend and Lore

*An Fathach agus An t-Iolar Buí*, The Eagle and the Giant, Margaret Cunningham, 29"x 48", naturally dyed and handspun yarns. This is the first tapestry Margaret spun, dyed and wove. It took her several months from start to finish. The theme is a blend of two local stories. One is the notion that Slieve League – the mountain range between Malinbeg and Teelin – is actually formed by a giant lying on its back. The second is about the eagle that swept up a little girl from Teelin and flew with her to Malinbeg, where the bird placed her down safely.

Many different versions of this story have survived the years. T.C. McGinely documented one such tale in 1867 from Nannie O'Byrne of Malinbeg, who claimed to be a direct descendant of the little girl swept up by the eagle. Apparently, the 2 ½-year-old Brigit was taken aloft over Slieve League while her mother was 'cheerfully employed behind her spinning wheel'. The eagle's claw marks could be seen on the little girl's shoulders throughout her life and even into her eighties, when she would 'occasionally exhibit them … for verification of her story'.

– *The Cliff Scenery of South West Donegal* by T.C.McGinley

Collection of Údarás na Gaeltachta, Barna, County Galway

Photo: Margaret Cunningham

*St Luke*, Dermot
Cannon, size 33"x46",
commercial yarn.

Collection of Taipéis
Gael

Photo: Margaret
Cunningham

*The Lion of St Mark*, Máire McGinely, 30"x 48", naturally dyed and handspun yarn. 'This tapestry was based on a page in the *Book of Kells*. I tried to imitate the colour of parchment with the natural coloured background. It was a complicated piece with all the detail'.

St Mark is one of the four evangelists in the Bible. St Jerome assigned attributes or symbols to them, linking Matthew with a winged man, Mark with a lion, John with an eagle, and Luke with an ox or calf. According to this theory, the man relates to the nativity; the lion represents royalty; the calf is a traditional sacrificial animal; and the soaring eagle is associated with the Ascension.

Collection of Michael O'Doherty

Photo: Máire McGinley

*Clann Lir*, Children of Lir, Conal McIntyre, 33"x 40", commercial yarn. 'Like in my tapestry, *Eye of the Ocean*, I am experimenting with movement in this piece'.

Collection of Joseph McGough

Photo: Conal McIntyre

*Children of Lir*, Dermot Cannon, 29"x 48", commercial and handspun yarn. This tapestry is based on the story of King Lir, whose jealous second wife, Aoife, cast a spell with a druid's wand on his lovely four children, banishing them to the community of swans for 900 years.

Collection of Noreen P. Denihan

Photo: Dermot Cannon

*Bonnán Buí*, Yellow Bittern, Margaret Cunningham, 4' x 4', commercial and handspun yarn. This piece is based on a poem by Cathal Buí Mac Giolla Gunna and is one Margaret had studied for her leaving certificate from secondary school. It is about a man who is suffering from alcoholism, whom the poet compares to a yellow bittern that dies from thirst beside a frozen pool. In the centre of the tapestry is a silhouette of a man pulling himself up from the ground. To the right of him is a bird lying dead beside frozen water.

'The musician in me appreciates this poem as it is also a song. Weaving it is another example of how my interests converge in tapestry. I enjoy abstract pieces. With this one, I explored more subtle colours than I usually work with. It's made from a paper collage, like *Trasna II*. The background is woven in diamond shapes, as I've done before to add texture'.

Collection of Joseph M. Murphy, Country Bank, Scarsdale, New York

Photo: Margaret Cunningham

*Split Tree*, Margaret Cunningham, 30"x 48", commercial yarns. This tapestry is based on the poem, *St Patrick and the Four Masters* by Charles Beamer, a writer from Texas who is now living in Ireland. Margaret particularly connected with stanza two of the poem:

*Perhaps the trees spoke first*

*during the migrations, the sunderings;*

*perhaps the first dialogues*

*about the web and spirit of earth and sky…*

'I pictured the tree in my grandmother's yard that we often gathered around for family photographs. It had just been split by storms that week – a direct dialogue between earth and sky. In Charles' poem, he also mentions Newgrange, the solstice, polished flagstones and a crow. And so I went from there in composing the design of this piece'. – Margaret Cunningham

'Margaret's vision for this tapestry transcends time and people, and she worked it together in such an original way. She is spontaneous, seemingly uncritical of herself, fresh'. – Charles Beamer

Collection of Alice and Charles Beamer

Photo: Mark Butler

*Alleluia*, Praise the Lord, Margaret Cunningham, 12"x 16", commercial yarn. Based on images from the *Book of Kells*.

Private collection

Photo: Taipéis Gael

# Cross-Cultural Expressions

*Bean Ag Iascaireacht*, Woman Fishing, Monica de Bath, 18"x 42", natural dyes and handspun yarn. This early tapestry by Monica, which bears an Irish title, evokes a Central American flair – inspired by Guatemalan weavers who came to Glencolmcille on an artist exchange. 'The tapestry also celebrates the resourcefulness of women in both Guatemala and Ireland, fending for themselves for food, especially in Ireland during the Famine. The head of the woman has a Celtic and African look, showing influences from my work in Zimbabwe'.

Collection Of Mesa Heanne

Photo: Monica de Bath

*Viking Symbols*, 36"x36", commercial yarn. This tapestry was a transnational exchange that brought together weavers from ten nationalities. It was a project between Taipéis Gael and Kulturkaeldren, a Danish weaving group that teaches refugees and immigrant women from places such as Sri Lanka, Japan, Hong Kong, United Arab Emirates, Philippines and various African countries. While in Denmark, Taipéis Gael weavers Monica de Bath, Margaret Cunningham, Sandra Mockler, Dermot Cannon, Conal Gilllespie and Máire McGinley helped to design this piece. The theme is Bronze Age artefacts – symbols common to all. Each artist wove one square. When Kulturkaeldren came to Ireland in May 1994, the tapestry was pieced together for the first time.

Collection of Taipéis Gael

Photo: Margaret Cunningham

*An Turas*, Pilgrimage, Margaret Cunningham, 22"x31", commercial yarn. 'The colours of this tapestry are those of New Mexico and Utah, woven after a trip there. I saw the same concentric spirals in the American Southwest rock art that we have here in Ireland. I've incorporated both colour and image into this piece, celebrating our local pilgrimage.

'When traveling the fifteen Colmcille stations, the pilgrims say prayers walking barefooted. On this tapestry you can see people moving, as well as the mapped route of the pattern, or path that they follow.

'I used a technique of weaving triangular shapes into the background, which not only adds interest and dimension, but also helps with elasticity and attaining straight edges'.

Collection of Priscilla Hagon

Photo: Margaret Cunningham

*Texas Commission*, Margaret Cunningham, 4' x 4', commercial yarn. 'I enjoyed this commission as I was free to design whatever I wished for this family from Texas, whose relatives are from Donegal. They sent me photographs of their landscape – the bushes and nice flowers around their home. This helped me choose the colours for this piece. They also sent me rock-art symbols from the Pecos area of Texas, which I incorporated beside images from Celtic rock art'.

Collection of Susan Gallagher and William Durham

Photo: Margaret Cunningham

*An Ciúin Aingean*,
Pacific Bound, Margaret
Cunningham, 24"x 24",
commercial yarn. 'I wove
this after my trip to
New Mexico. Part of the
design was inspired by a
tourist guidebook I saw
there. I liked the vertical
lines of the trees against
the stream'.

Collection of Taipéis Gael

Photo: Margaret
Cunningham

*Rockies*, Margaret
Cunningham,
16"x14", commercial
yarn. 'This is another
tapestry inspired
by my trip to the
American West
and flying over the
continental divide'.

Collection of Taipéis
Gael

Photo: Margaret
Cunningham

# Tools

# Whorls

The Irish National Museum is home to a collection of yarn-spinning tools called hand spindles. A spindle consists of a shaft, or stick, which is a bit longer and wider than a pencil. Most have a whorl, or disc, attached to one end. Some spindles twirl in mid-air while dangling from a thread. Others are supported on the ground or by one's knee. The whorl acts like a flywheel and keeps the spindle turning. Whorls can be thick or thin, spherical, round or cross-slated.

In Ireland's past, spindle shafts were typically made of yew wood – *úir* in Irish. The whorls were made of bone and stone, often from oxen or sandstone. These transportable tools allow one to create yarn while doing other things simultaneously: herding sheep, cooking or chasing toddlers. Despite advances in spinning technology, the hand spindle is still used in many parts of the world.

Some of the whorls I examined at the National Museum were plain; others were decorated with perforations, incised lines and circles, or spirals like those on pre-Christian stonework. The weight of the whorl determines the type of fibre best suited for the spindle. Lighter whorls spin fibres with shorter staple lengths and finer hairs. Thus, cotton and a short-fibred sheep fleece, such as a Soay, should be spun with a lighter whorl than that which is used for spinning Scottish Blackface sheep fibres.

According to E. Charles Nelson and Wendy F. Walsh in *Trees of Ireland,* fossilized seeds of yew are found in peat deposits that date back to 8–9,000 years ago.[1] Many yew trees live to be over 2,000 years old. The yew was prominent in the Stone Age as a durable, versatile wood, often with a red hue and marked with knots. It polishes well, bends without breaking and was favoured for long bows. Its berries are 'sweet and innocent', yet its leaves are poisonous. Apparently, the mother of all Irish yew trees grows in Florencecourt, County Fermanagh, on the west side of Lough Erne.

It is an ancient Celtic belief that trees were not merely natural objects, but signs of the connectedness of heaven and earth. Yew was the sacred tree of the Irish druids. They believed the tree could transcend time and guard the doorway between this world and the next. 'Druids made wands from yew and kindled their fires with it', says John Matthews, in *The Druid Source Book.*[2] In legends around the world, wands or staffs of yew were considered especially potent. They could channel the spirit of the tree, the might of the gods, and the will of the owner.

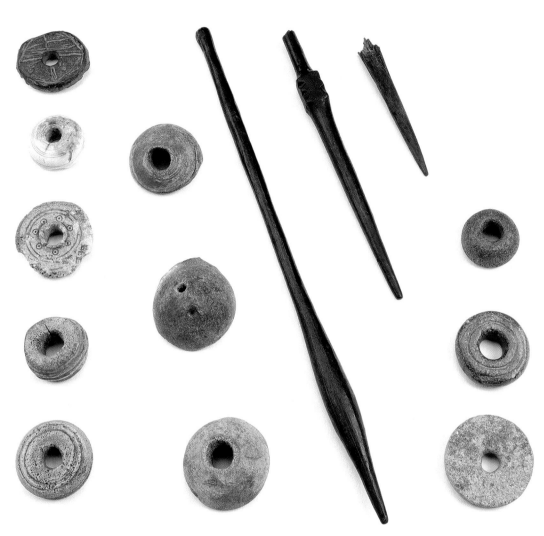

These spindle whorls and shafts were preserved in Irish bogs and now live in the National Museum of Ireland. The whorls are made of bone and sandstone.

The spindle shafts are sticks of yew. Often the whorls were inscribed with concentric circles or dots. When spun, the whorls with the concentric design give a pleasing visual effect. If any designs were carved into the wood shafts, they've since worn away. The three whorls on the right were found in Donegal bogs.

Photo: National Museum of Ireland

I wondered as I looked at the artefacts in the National Museum, if it would be far fetched to infer that some of these yew and spiral-decorated spindles could have belonged to a druid.

Assuming the museum would not be keen to allow me to experiment with their spindle artefacts, I decided to commission a carpenter to make me a spindle shaft of yew. Ollie Burke from Galway rose to the challenge. He whittled, smoothed and polished a yew spindle as close in size and shape as possible to the prehistoric ones dug from the bogs. Afterwards, I paid a visit to a stonemason, Dennis Groggin, who cut for me a sandstone whorl and decorated it with an endless spiral. I put the two together and spun wool from a Blackface and a Galway sheep. The size and weight of the whorl seemed perfect for both. However, the Soay demanded more from me as a spinner. The weight of the whorl threatened to snap my thread at any irregular movement or inattention.

As I plied, the inscribed circle on my replicated whorl spun a pleasing visual spiral dance. I wondered if this ancient design on whorls was meant to be intentional – invoking a journey inward or outward. Is there a connection between the spiral and druid worship? Does the design reflect what the Greeks believed about fate – that it was a spun thread; that both thread and time were linear, both easily and arbitrarily broken? This concentric design could well embrace what Elizabeth Wayland Barber says in *Women's Work: The First 20,000 Years* about the common ancient association of the world regarding the notion that spinning is the creation of new life. 'Women create thread', she states. 'They somehow pull it out of nowhere, just as they produce babies out of nowhere'.[3] This point is further illustrated with the fact that the word 'spin' did not originally mean to turn or to twirl, but was derived from the word 'span' – to draw out, stretch long. Hence, the term 'lifespan', which brings us back around to the notion of fate.

There are documented connections between druids and the Greeks. John Matthews cites sources that suggest this. The origin of druidism was written about in Diogenes Laertius's *Lives of the Philosophers*. Apparently Julius Caesar knew a druid named Divitiacus. In a great rebellion during Caesar's time it was said that 'Druids uttered no word against Caesar or for him'.[4]

Another excerpt from Matthews' book that sheds light on ancient druid and Greek connections takes us further back in time. The passage mentions a person named Iobarth, who left Ireland to settle in the northern islands of Greece and befriended the Athenians. He was from the people of the Tuatha Dé, who possessed 'power in every art and every druidic occultism'. Through druidry, the Athenians apparently learned from Iobarth to form demon-spirits in the bodies of the soldiers of the Athenians who were slain, so that they were fit for battle again.[5]

Maybe it was the druids who planted the notion of spinning one's fate in the minds of the Greeks in the first place. What does all of this musing about whorls, yew trees, druids and Greeks lead to? If ever you give a woman a spindle and a sack of Irish wool with which she will spin your fate, choose that of a Blackface sheep over a Soay. Its locks are longer and more coarse, and so the spinner will be less likely to break the thread.

# Wheels: James Shiels, Master Spinning-Wheelwright

The home of the late James Shiels stands a stone's throw from St Patrick's Cross in the town of Carndonagh, County Donegal. Like one of the three pilgrims chiselled into the base of the sculptured seventeenth-century cross, I journeyed to the Inishowen Peninsula a few years before Mr Shiels' death, to visit the last master spinning-wheelwright in Ireland.

The mahogany front door of Mr Shiels' house stood open to Bridge Street in a welcome gesture to anyone who might happen upon it. From the street, sunlight streamed inside and down the front hall to the threshold of his workshop, which was framed with raincoats and knee-high Wellingtons. The room overflowed with wood chippings and spinning-wheel parts: turned legs, clusters of flyers that hung from the ceiling including skeins of wool, bobbins in various stages of completion, iron rods, bits of leather and foot treadles. A few antique wheels fixed to the wall collected dust – vestiges of wheels made by James' father or uncles.

I was delighted to meet Mr Shiels. About a year had passed since I had asked him to build me a spinning wheel like the one my ancestors used in Donegal. Our agreement of sale was made through two letters that crossed the Atlantic many months before, a mutual leap of faith that was sealed like a handshake.

When I arrived at his home, James had three spinning wheels waiting for me to try, two made of teak and one of mahogany. I sat down to treadle the teak wheel first. This smooth-finished wheel felt solid underfoot, as if it would outlast the more lightweight, contemporary wheel I use at home. I tried to spin some of the merino and silk wool that I often keep with me. But it was too delicate and slippery for the wheel's draw, or for 'the swallow', as James said. So he carded a handful of Suffolk-crossbreed fleece for me to spin. This wool, which is more coarse and thicker in staple, glided from hand to bobbin with only the slightest pull and tug.

Greasing the movable parts of the mahogany wheel with Vaseline – James's standard oiling remedy – he said, 'This wheel is actually a flax wheel. It is called the Dutch Wheel or Scotch Wheel. It came from Holland to Scotland then to Ireland in the eighteenth century and was used for flax'.

He took the bobbin to a circular blade to widen its groove a sliver and told me to give this richly grained wheel a try. It treadled more easily than the teak wheel and it swallowed the wool from my hands effortlessly. Within minutes I fell in love with it. I spent the better part of the next hour spinning and chatting with James.

'I learned to make wheels from my father. He used a treadle-powered lathe that my brother and I pumped while he worked'.

He said that his father's spinning wheels sold like mad during World War II because store-bought yarn was difficult to find. 'People living near the beaches used to salvage timber from boats that had been torpedoed near Malin Head and the Isle of Doagh'.

According to David Shaw-Smith in *Ireland's Traditional Crafts,* in those days spinning studios in Donegal had up to forty-five wheels going at once. More than a century before – in the eighteenth century – the introduction of this wheel into Donegal homes changed the social pattern of the country side:

'It was light in weight, easily transported and it became customary for the young women of a parish to gather in a different house each night for communal spinning . . . called the "factory".' [6]

After World War II, James said, 'You couldn't give a spinning wheel away'. I recalled what Jimmy Carr, a retired weaver and contemporary of Mr Shiels, had explained to me about the similar decline of spinning on the west coast of Donegal.

'Homespun started back up in 1940. It came back at that time, yeah. The fabric and cloth was very scarce. When the war was over the homespun kind of died out here, you see. People left for Scotland, England, America, all over. No help in the houses to do the homespun'.

In the 1960s James Shiels started making spinning wheels again. His son Johnny began helping him in the seventies, followed by his son Charles in the eighties. He gained recognition and was asked to show the wheels at museums and heritage centres. At this time he also began receiving inquiries from people who had seen his wheels and wanted them for furniture. So James designed several wheels with lamps attached to the distaff (a staff attached to the spinning wheel that holds unspun wool).

'Why not add book holders so people could read while they spin?' I asked. 'Or make them with drink holders like the kind installed in cars?'

'With long straws', James added with a sense of humour that became more apparent when he talked about an Irish television production that had featured himself, his apprentice-son Charles and his wife Kathleen.

'This documentary, *Hands*, by David Shaw-Smith, featured traditional Irish craftsmen. A cameraman spent several weeks with us filming Charles and me in the woodshop and Kathleen spinning'. James slipped the documentary into the VCR while Mrs Shiels served tea and biscuits.

'He made me carry that piece of wood into my shop several times before I got it right', James grinned.

The late master spinning-wheelwright James Shiels of Carandonagh, Co. Donegal, making adjustments to the device on this traditional Donegal Wheel, which will move the flywheel forward and back. Using teak or mahogany, James made replicas of the Dutch Wheel, originally a flax wheel imported to Ireland from Holland in the eighteenth century to foster the linen trade. Over time, spinners and wheelwrights modified it for wool.

'See there', Kathleen said, pointing to the image on the television screen, 'those are my feet treadling!' She laughed. 'You know, he spent five or six hours filming me spinning for my two-minute debut'.

'I looked better then, didn't I?' James said, a man then in his sixties.

'But not more distinguished', I assured him.

While the documentary filled the living room with images of turned legs, wood chips and bobbins, I asked James and Kathleen for spinning songs and folklore that they could remember from their youth. Kathleen recalled, 'In the olden days, a girl who tied a red ribbon around the flax on her distaff meant she was looking for a partner'. Her story gives life to an anecdote mentioned by David Shaw-Smith: When the work [spinning] was finished the girls were usually joined by the young men of the parish, and the night ended with a dance. As the saying goes, 'Many's the match was made at the factory'.[7]

James Shiels did not let on that his reputation extended across the county and beyond. Only after meeting other spinners and weavers in Ireland did this become clear to me, 'How is James?' people would say. 'I must visit him myself'.

As James poured me a third cup of tea, I settled into my chair, honoured to be there, thrilled to have come all this way for a wheel and to hear James' stories.

'At one time, I used to make miniature wheels and be on the road selling them', he said. 'But not anymore. People come to me now'.

Later, James carried my spinning wheel down Bridge Street to where I had parked my car, a stone's throw from St Patrick's Cross. As we tucked the wheel into the back seat, I felt a twinge of sadness. My pilgrimage was over and I was sorry to say goodbye.

# Raw Materials

# Sheep and Wool

The two most widely raised sheep in Donegal, according to Seán O'Donnell of the Carrick Sheep Mart, are Cheviot and Scottish Blackface mountain sheep. These are the two breeds that weavers Máire McGinley and Dermot Cannon raise.

Cheviots, whose wool is used in the tweed trade, originated in the Cheviot Hills on the border of England and Scotland in the 1700s and do well in windswept conditions. These sheep have upright ears, black muzzles and feet, and wool-free faces and legs. Their long locks are soft against the skin and have a helical crimp, which makes the wool resilient. They are reportedly active and alert. My impression of them, however, after watching a friend's flock at home, is that they seem scared of almost everything. But a recent pubic radio programme, which reported on a study published in the journal *Nature*, claims, 'Sheep may have gotten a bad rap'. The findings indicated that sheep may tend to get too easily dismissed. Says Dr Keith Kendrick, one of the authors of the sheep intelligence study, 'Any animal, including humans, once they are scared, don't tend to show signs of intelligent behavior'.[1]

This notion that sheep haven't been given due credit lives in Glencolmcille as well. 'Ah, they're smart', Anthony Boyle (weaver Margaret Cunningham's uncle) said to me on the roadside one evening as he was feeding his flock of Scottish Blackface, Cheviot and cross-breeds. 'They recognize the sound of my tractor when I round the bend. They come running. Humans are the dumbest of animals …'

*Nature* also says sheep are smarter than we think. A study conducted at the Babraham Institute in Cambridge found that they can discriminate between very similar countenances (such as between flock members) and remember up to fifty faces for two years.

This finding explains why my sheep come to me but run from my husband – as it is he who wrestles them to the ground when it's time to clip their hooves. But it refutes an early twentieth-century anecdote about the custom of shepherds fooling their sheep. According to the anecdote, when the shepherds wanted to rest they would hang their cloaks on their crooks so that they could lie down without being missed by their sheep. Clearly someone had it all wrong. The sheep huddled beside their shepherd not because they mistook the cloak and staff for their caretaker, but rather to protect him from possible wolves while he snoozed. So it seems sheep are quite considerate animals, too.

*Tread Caoraigh*, Flock of Sheep, Conal Gillespie, 28"x 50," natural dyes and handspun yarn.

Collection of Michael Herity

Photo: Conal Gillespie

Scottish Blackface sheep are one of the most numerous breeds in the United Kingdom. They came originally from the north of England, spread to the Highlands of Scotland by the middle of the eighteenth century and eventually slipped into the north of Ireland. This small-horned breed is a result of selective breeding since medieval times with a short, coarse-wooled ancestor. Today their wool is medium length and more suitable for carpet yarns than clothes. Some claim that this wool's natural springiness enables carpets made with it to bounce back after pressure from feet and furniture. Having worked with this wool, I have to disagree. I've found it a bit brittle and lifeless – good for wall-to-wall carpeting, or perhaps saddle blankets, but not suited for a soft pile rug. It is also good for tapestry though it does not take up dyes as brightly as wool from other breeds.

Less commonly raised sheep in Donegal are the Galway and Soay, which are presently listed by the Rare Breeds Survival Trust (United Kingdom) as endangered in Ireland. Deborah Robson, editor of *Handspun Treasures from Rare Breeds,* writes:

> Sheep were originally domesticated 15,000 years ago, along with the goat, the dog, and the reindeer. Yet the idea of rare breeds of any type has only arisen in the last twenty years, in terms of organized effort to preserve genetic potential, and perhaps in the last one hundred,

in terms of dawning awareness that individual breeds were at risk.

Economic pressure promotes a handful of breeds at the expense of the rest. In the matter of wool, medium grade fibre [length and thickness of hair follicles] has dominated the economic system since the industrial equipment started producing more textiles than craft workers did. Today [as in Ireland], the economic status of many sheep breeds is described in terms of meat production, with the adjunct comment that wool is 'acceptable' or 'adequate'. [2]

Any handspinner raising a flock would aim for *exquisite,* which is what the fleeces of both the Soay and Galway sheep are.

The Soay have been called the only living example of the small primitive sheep that inhabited the British Isles before the coming of the Norsemen and the Romans. They came originally from the island of Soay off the coast of Scotland. These sheep have thick, large horns in comparison to their relatively small bodies. Their primitive features include a short tail and coloured fleece, which undergoes an annual moult. Most Soays have a white belly like wild sheep. The fact that Soays retain this feature shows how truly primitive the breed is. The fleece is double coated, with extremely soft fibres mixed with coarser longer 'guard hairs', which help wick away the dirt and rain. Often the entire fleece is soft and difficult to distinguish between inner and outer coats. These sheep are usually a mix of light and dark brown wool.

The Dublin textile designer Mary O'Rourke (who had attended one of Taipéis Gael's natural dye workshops), raises Soay sheep on her farm in the Dublin Mountains. She spins lustrous yarns suitable for personal wear from their wool. Mary said that for years after this wool is spun it retains 'a wonderful hold, a glisten of lanolin and a vibrancy to the hand'. But she admits it is a lot of work collecting the locks from hedges and fence posts each spring when it is shed. She keeps the Soay breed for conservation reasons and worries that interests in Dublin to make a 'park' for city dwellers out of the mountains where she lives will limit the commonage areas upon which she and others have let their sheep graze for centuries. A park would contribute to the endangerment of the breed.

The Galway sheep is found mainly in Counties Galway, Roscommon, Mayo, Clare, Westmeath and Offaly, reported Anne-Marie Moroney in *Spin Off* magazine.[3] Galway sheep are a large-framed, white-wooled, hornless breed with wool on their foreheads. They are reportedly docile animals, which is what I found when I visited Theresa O'Donohue's flock just outside of Doolin in County Clare.

I took to these sheep immediately as they resemble my own Romneys. Their hair is long, lustrous and soft enough to wear (even softer than a Romney) and would knit up nicely for Aran sweaters. Developed in the late eighteenth century, Galway

sheep were a cross-breed with Dishley Leicester rams, probably owing their lustre to the Leicester.

On my second visit with Theresa, it was springtime and her four ewes had seven lambs between them. She said that an average fleece weighed in at 8–12 lb, quite large compared to the Cheviot, Scottish Blackface and Soay. Theresa gave me one of the fleeces to take home with me.

Ever since, I have enjoyed spinning with this versatile fleece and weaving it into tapestries. I look forward to knitting with it. As one of sixteen endangered flocks registered in the United Kingdom, Theresa's Galway sheep in Doolin contribute to maintaining diversity in wool – colours and textures – essential to preserving the full range of skills and cultural values embodied in textile art and craft.

Spinning with fleeces indigenous to Ireland, Taipéis Gael not only increases the demand for variety in wool, but, more importantly, it celebrates rare breeds and helps save them from oblivion.

Dermot Cannon, of Straboy townland, stands in the middle of Scottish Blackfaced mountain sheep and Cheviots.

A Cheviot ewe and her lamb.

Dermot Cannon, holding *diemheas*, traditional shears, as he waits to board a craft bound for a shearing on Rathlin O'Beirne Island. His shears are almost exactly like those made in medieval times. A glimpse of artifacts in M.L. Ryder's book, *Sheep and Man*, shows a similar pair in the Devizes Museum in Fryfield Wiltshire. In the Bronze Age, knives were used to pluck wool because many breeds then still moulted. Bronze is less elastic than iron; so a continuous tool – as the one shown in this photo – was not possible to make. Artifacts from 1000 B.C. show shears made of two knives connected by a spring.

Malinbeg locals heading to Rathlin O'Beirne Island for a sheep shearing. This *uig*, harbour, is the only boat port in Malinbeg.

'In ainm an athair, agus an mhac agus an spoiraid naomh, amen. In the name of the father and of the son and of the holy spirit amen'. Paddy O'Gara leads the blessing before Conal McGinley (cap in hand) and others set out to sea. The current between the mainland and this most western island of Donegal is always strong. They will ride the backs of swells and fall into deep furrows en route to Rathlin O'Beirne Island for a sheep shearing.

Disembarking on the island can be treacherous. Conal McGinley recalls the time he took his flock to the island for grazing and a Blackface sheep caught its horn on the rung of the ladder leading up the cliff. The sea lowered and so did the boat, leaving the cloven-hooved creature there to dangle. Again came a swell to lift the boat, and finally Conal was able to rescue the animal.

Lighthouse on Rathlin O'Beirne Island.

Old walls on Rathlin O'Beirne Island serve as a sheepfold in which to shear sheep. This flock is made up of Cheviot and Scottish Blackface mountain sheep.

Reaping the wool harvest on Rathlin O'Beirne Island.

A local technique:
'Shear the belly first,
then tie the forelegs
and one back leg'.
Dermot Cannon

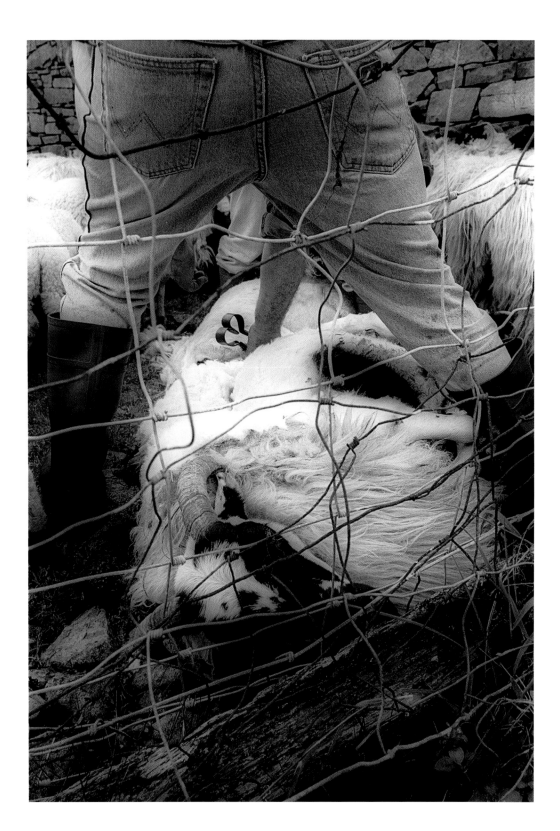

*Weaving Tapestry in Rural Ireland*

Máire McGinley's
husband, Conal,
dipping sheep on
Rathlin O'Beirne
Island as a precaution
against ticks and other
parasites.

Remains of a monastic
site on Rathlin
O'Beirne Island
ascribed to Assiscus, a
favourite disciple of St
Patrick. Archaeologist
Michael Herity informs
us in his book,
*Gleanncholmcille: A
Guide to 5000 Years of
History in Stone*, that
Assiscus had been a
hermit on this island
for seven years when
his monks removed
him forcibly and took
him to the mainland.
Local tradition adds
that Assiscus paused
for a last look at his
beloved hermitage,
and as he lost sight of
it forever, he cried. To
this day, water springs
up in a well there from
his tears.

Conal McGinley pours
water into an ancient
lichen-covered bowl…

….so that Sheila,
who has worked hard
rounding up the sheep,
can have a drink.

Sean Murrin and Sheila leaving Rathlin O'Byrne Island with a sack of wool.

Sean Murrin heading for the boat below with a 67 lb sack of wool that will eventually be sold in Letterkenny.

Mark Tubridy helps load a bale of wool onto the boat bound for Malinbeg.

Tossing bales of wool to the stairs below, where they will be loaded onto the boat bound for Malinbeg on the mainland.

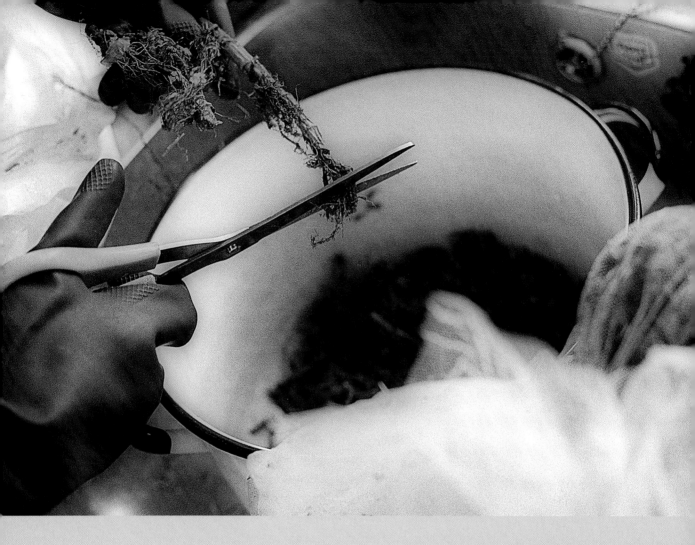

# Natural Dyes

# Natural Dyes

For centuries, the sea is where weavers in Ireland have gone to collect material for dyes. It is where they go to peel lichen and dog whelks from rocks, gather bladder and egg wrack from the shores, and collect bracken and heather from the headlands above. The sea is where Taipéis Gael weavers go to begin making natural dyes.

The earliest traces of naturally-dyed textiles in Ireland reach back to about 700 BC according to Maria Fitzgerald, who received her doctorate in Textile Production in Prehistoric and Early Medieval Ireland. Fitzgerald said evidence of spinning and natural dyes also appears in the early Irish Brehon laws that delineated which colours could be used by which classes. Laws were also created to protect the weavers and their materials, such as those that ensured the weavers' right to grow madder (a plant whose roots yield a red dye) in home gardens, and those that permitted women to use spindles as weapons.[1] Similarly, a traditional Irish law suggests that it was once a priority to safeguard the community's homegrown dye plants, 'There are three tresspasses of a hen in a herb garden: the soft-swallowing of bees, injury to the dye plants, and attack on garlic. A guilty hen shall have her feet tied together, or rag boots put on'.[2]

The significance of dyeing in Irish history is also demonstrated in the book of Lismore, believed to have been written by the early fifteenth century. It contains a passage about the sixth-century St Ciaran, and his mother – a dyer – who tells her son to leave the house because it was said to be unlucky to have men around while dyeing. However, St Ciaran got angry and cursed the cloth so that it dyed unevenly. Eventually, after his mother pleaded with him to remove the curse, he did so, but only to turn the dye into bleach. Again his mother pleaded with him, this time asking him to bless the blue dye. St Ciaran agreed, but his blessing made it so that anything that touched her cloth – dogs, cats, trees – turned blue as well.

More recent writing that supports the history of the use of natural dyes in Ireland includes a discussion on an archaeological site in which madder seeds were found in a hearth at Boho, County Fermanagh.[3] Others note the ruins of dye huts on Iniskea, County Mayo, which contained middens with dog whelk shells (more commonly associated with the purple dye of the Phoenicians made in the Eastern Mediterranean), and several shellfish midden sites found along the coast from County Clare to Donegal, most of them falling within the early Christian period.[4]

The results of a dye workshop. Except for the cochineal and indigo, the dye materials were reaped from the Irish land and sea.

Left to right: knotted egg wrack (sea weed), madder root overdyed with heather (russet), cochineal (magenta), indigo (blues), indigo overdyed with gorse (blue-green), gorse (gold), peat (light brown), natural wool.

The study of names in connection with the history of Irish dyeing practices is important to help document the old ways and reveal aspects of past culture. For instance, the word for dyestuffs in the Book of Leinster is *ruaman* with the root word *ruam* (red), which reinforces the idea that the Celts loved bright colours.[5] Another interesting fact is that Gaelic plant names have regional variations. The names can be descriptive such as 'the three leaved plant', or can be simple translations of its common English name such as *rós na con* for dog rose. Gaelic names can refer to the use of the plant, its colour or even its supposed mystical properties. As an example, woad, which is a blue dye, can be called *guirmrean*, the blue one, or *glas lus*, pale blue weed.[6] Purple loosestrife obviously had important powers for it was known as *lus an sith chainnt*, the peace-making plant. Similarly, place names sometimes also refer to dyes such as *Creagacorcrona*, Crag of the Purple Dyestuff, on Slyne Head in Connemara, and *Strathnacorcorcracha*, Wall of the Purple Dyestuff, in Gweedore, County Donegal.[7]

As with many things in Ireland, dyestuffs hold a strong link with the supernatural world. In Uíbh Ráthach, Contae Chiarraí (County Kerry), writer Bríd Mahon says, 'they never let children wear white underclothes lest they be swept away by the *púcaí* and as a safeguard they picked *sceochan na gcloch* to dye the garment yellowish-brown'.[8]

Likewise, dyers of old had reputations as herbal healers since many dyestuffs were also used for folk medicines. Perhaps the leftover stems, petals and leaves of medicinal plants would have been tossed into the dyepot for the later purpose of reaping colours.

# A Dyer's Journal

On the strand in Glencolmcille opposite Taipéis Gael's first studio in Oideas Gael, I found that soft things lashed at hard things: waves crashed into rocks, sun-coloured lichens chewed granite, and snails bore holes into the backs of mollusks. From dune to dune plant hues varied in intensity and tone, like the tunes played by local fiddlers. Bladder wrack, with its million green air sacs that keep it afloat, crackled beneath the weight of my foot on the sand.

It was a blustery autumn morning, and I had gathered with ten textile artists on the beach at low tide. Our group included Monica de Bath, the cooperative's founder; weavers Margaret Cunningham and Máire McGinley; Taipéis Gael mentors Jimmy Carr and Rose Hegarty; a horticulturist, Larry Brownen from Offaly; a Dublin textile designer, Mary O'Rourke; the then president of the Guild of Irish Spinners and Weavers, Mary Shiels; Ann Adams, an American tapestry weaver from Moscow, Idaho and myself.

Taipéis Gael Founder Monica de Bath tossing dyer's chamomile into the dyepot outside their first studio at Oideas Gael Cultural College.

We fanned out with buckets and plastic bags to collect seaweed and to scrape and pick lichens and dog whelks from the rocks. We then took our bounty back to Taipéis Gael's studio to experiment with these native dye materials. For the next two days we pored over dye recipes from books and from Jimmy Carr's and Rose Hegarty's memories. With Larry Brownen's help we identified native plants from land and sea and discussed their Latin, common and Irish names. We sniffed, chopped and brewed.

With nearly everyone speaking in both Irish and English, our workshop echoed the craft classes offered in Irish by the Congested Districts Board at the beginning of the last century in the nearby towns of Carrick, Kilcar and Killybegs, in which the words *dúlamán* (seaweed), *crotal* (lichens), *fraoch* (heather) and *buachallán buí* (ragwort) – some of the dyestuffs with which we experimented that day – would have been recognized by all.

Our workshop produced a bouquet of yarns dyed with heather, madder, gorse, bracken, cochineal, bladder wrack, purple loosestrife, lady's bedstraw, ragwort and bogbean. All of these are discussed in detail in the following glossary of dyes.

*Pucan*, Galway Hooker,
Máire McGinley,
2.5'x4', commercial
and handspun wool.
A commission by a
family that sails.

Collection of Margaret
O'Driscoll.

Photo: Máire McGinley

# A Glossary of Dyes

In the following section Irish dye plants and materials are described by their physical characteristics and the colours they yield. Following each definition is additional information that includes anecdotes or lore about the use of these plants as dyes or medicines, as well as some of my own experiences in collecting and experimentation.

## Dyes from the Sea

**Bladder** and **Knotted Egg Wrack** (*Fucus vesiculosus* and *Ascophyllum nodosum*).
Bladder wrack is a dark green plant with tiny air sacs and a leafy construction. Knotted egg wrack is a mix of colours, from lima-bean green to shades of brown and orange. Its sacks are larger and fewer and have a more rubber-like texture than bladder wrack. Both yield a rich brown dye. The seaweeds mentioned below that I researched gave colours ranging from beige to honey, shades that one could find among fleeces of undyed wool.

In an article entitled 'Wrack and Wreck' in *Irish Folkways*, E. Estyn Evans reminds us that there isn't any part of Ireland that is more than sixty miles from the sea; that the feeding value of nob wrack, which grows toward the high-tide mark, is almost equal to that of meadow hay; and that certain species of seaweed are still gathered for human consumption, including carrigeen or Irish moss, sloke or laver, dulse and *dúlamán*. Evans found that in 1830, when the potatoes gave out, many people went to the seaside to gather *dúlamán*.

Evans also mentions that, back in 1750, Donegal tenants paid their rent in kelp, and that 'any surplus was bartered for "the two luxuries" – spirits and tobacco – enjoyed by men and women alike'. He also says that there is an art to reaping the kelp, that even the breezes play a role. 'An offshore wind is needed because it is the returning undertow which brings deeper weeds ashore'. But for the wrack, he emphasizes, 'every bay has its own particular wind'. Among the seaweeds Evans mentions that are good for food and fodder are the wracks – knotted and bladder.[1]

Heinrich Becker assembled a collection of stories and anecdotes from his trip to Ireland called *Seaweed Memories*. 'Curing Skin Disease by Bladderwrack', written by Michael Ó Donnchada of Inis Oirr, shares a bladder wrack recipe that is an antidote

for healing. He says, 'When the seaweed would be well boiled and well mixed . . . and a kind of jelly made of it, a poultice of seaweed and juice . . . it should be rubbed on the skin to take care of rashes'. It worked for a Connemara man who thrice visited hospitals in Galway and Dublin to no avail before consulting a local woman of wisdom on these matters.[2]

Marine biologists Lorna Kelly and Jim Morrissey of the Irish Seaweed Association, housed in the Marine Science Institute at NUI Galway, share a dyer's appreciation of seaweed. I visited them one afternoon after having filled a trash bag with seaweed from the strand in Salthill just outside Galway. I thought I had chosen three or four different kinds – the same species of seaweed on which I had experimented with Taipéis Gael, and others I had yet to try.

'Oh, they're *beautiful*', Lorna said, lifting the weeds from my sack as if I'd just given her a bouquet of rare orchids. She placed the slimy, sandy clump into a large, 3-inch-deep pan of water so that the plants would untangle without tearing. I could not help but juxtapose this image with that of the bulldozers I had just seen on the shores, pushing back the often pungent and fly-ridden red and black weed into heaps so that pedestrians could enjoy the strand.

Lorna's gentleness with the delicate 'sea vegetables', as she called them, was touching. I soon learned that I had collected nine – not three as I had thought earlier – species of *vegetable:* tangle or oar weed (dark green that reminds me of a grass skirt); sugar kelp (brownish-orange); dillisk or dulce (red); fucus (light green that looked indistinguishable to me from serrated wrack); carrigeen (red with beige tips); and one whose common name I never caught, but looked just like *criptoplura rimosa* and *plumaria elegans.*

Most of the seaweed biomass in the North Atlantic is provided by the kelps, wracks and red algae. The Seaweed Institute validates what E. Estyn Evans says regarding *ascophyllum* being fed to animals, also adding that it is the most economically important wrack in the area. Most of the harvestable quantities are found along the intertidal coast from Galway to Donegal. Though I've seen no published evidence proving that wracks were historically used for dyes in Ireland, I believe that it is likely to have been so.

In 1996, Michael D. Guiry of the Irish Seaweed Association identified a few problems in the industry, including a shortage of entrepreneurs to help with the growth and development of the field.[3] After reading this, I could not help but wonder if the Irish Seaweed Association should link up with Údarás na Gaeltachta and the Irish Heritage Council to initiate a natural dye industry for local wool. Perhaps both land and sea products would benefit, as the price per pound for raw Irish wool cannot sink much lower than present rates. Surely yarn dyed with the heather of the Irish hills and weeds from the sea would appeal to textile people the world over. Years ago – after dumping a load of naturally dyed yarns on his desk in his Barna office – I mentioned this idea to Pádraig Ó hAoláin at Údarás na Gaeltachta, who listened politely and then offered to give me a grant for a book, which is how this project began.

**Dog whelks** (*Nucella lapillus*), of the family *Muricidae.* 'Dog whelks are often confused with winkles', said Dr Martin McNulty, a marine biologist at NUI Galway. 'The difference is the dog whelk shell is not rounded or continuous, there is a groove on the underside and often the whelks can be white'. A visit to his dissection lab showed the hypobranchial gland of the whelk, a fingernail-sized half moon of a thing, which secretes the purple dye.

The Marine Science Centre reports that as of 2006 dog whelks are not listed as an endangered species in Ireland. This is valuable to know as it takes approximately 12,000 to make an ounce of dye. One ounce will easily colour a pound of wool, which, after being spun, is enough for a child's sweater.

Gathering whelks is no picnic. It is a tide-dependent game in which the whelks manage to wedge themselves deep into crevices on coastal rocks. My fingers become scraped and cold while working. To collect 12,000 whelks would take hours, thus the work is quite labour intensive for just one sweater. This is one reason why in the past – besides the invention of synthetic dyes in the mid-nineteenth century – purple was usually worn only by royalty or clergy, and why the dye huts along the west coast of Ireland now lie in ruin.

A note about their collection: these snails lay their eggs inland, so the larger adults tend to be found further out in the water. Whelks also prefer salt water to fresh and therefore should be more abundant farther away from where a river meets the sea. Autumn is reported to be the best time for harvesting whelks for dyes as the snails' energies go toward reproduction in the spring, and therefore, their dye propensities may suffer.

In the dye workshop I attended at Taipéis Gael, we had hoped to achieve a purple dye from dog whelks. Immersing about seven lb of whelks in simmering water for about two to four hours with sodium diothionite, a reducing agent, produced only a faint lavender on wool, which washed off. On paper, a swipe of snail secretion had turned purple after twenty-four hours. This suggests further experimentation with whelks on linen.

Some studies have shown that the Irish dog whelk is an indigoid dye and calls for an alkaline dyebath in order to dissolve the whelk's purple dye molecules. Urine – with its ammonia-like properties – is a choice liquid for this purpose. Historically, dyers have used urine, since it costs nothing and is always available. However, we chose not to try this recipe during our workshop for fear the 'fragrance' would chase away Liam Ó Cuinneagáin's students, who were brushing up on their Irish in the classrooms downstairs.

**Rock lichens** (*Xanthoria parietina*), *corcir, corcur* in Irish. Orange growths that are found on coastal rocks. Their colour is owed to parietinic acid and can turn shades of purple if steeped for about three weeks in alkali.

Su Grierson comments that lichens have been used in dyes, perfumes, paints, medicines – including antibiotics – embalming fluid, and in food for man and beast.

In her book *Lichens For Vegetable Dyeing*, Eileen M. Bolton states that lichens can be used as a mordant, 'Cloth receiving this kind of dye [purple from whelks] was often coloured with a preparation made from two kinds of lichens in the Levant . . . When the art of making the famous Tyrian purple died out, the lichen alone was used for making regal purple. This preparation for lichens is referred to as Argol, Archl or Orchil'. It seems the recipe for this process made its way from the Levant to Italy then on to England around the fourteenth century.[4]

Crustaceous lichens are said to have been the first plants on earth, corroding rocks to create soil. Because they take generations to grow and many species are endangered, it is more environmentally friendly to make purple dye with a combination of indigo and madder or cochineal, especially if dyeing large quantities of wool.

I have learned many things from my experience with lichens, including some techniques that have proven successful. For instance, the best method for removing lichen from a rock – a nearly impossible feat – is to scrape them off with a sharp knife after they are swollen from rain. However, in experimenting with new techniques, there are always failures, such as the time my dye pot of lichens – which had been soaking in urine for six weeks – flipped over in a fierce Galway windstorm (coincidentally, it was the same storm that had cracked weaver Margaret Cunningham's grandmother's tree, the subject of her tapestry, *Split Tree*).

## Dyes from the Land

**Bogbean** (*Menyanthes trifoliata*), *bearnan lachan* in Irish. This plant produces bright pink and white flowers in May and June. The roots give a brown dye while its leaves yield a yellow-green.

Bogbean has been known for centuries for its medicinal purposes, and, as Jimmy Carr once mentioned to me, 'It was brewed as a drink for the blood'.

Looking at the brownish-green dye results on Taipéis Gael's yarn, mentor Rose Hegarty suggested, 'The colour's no better than the taste'.

**Bracken** (*Pteridium aquilinum*), *raithneach* in Irish. A fern growing in woods and on barren mountains, which gives a yellow-orange dye.

**Gorse**, **whin**, **furze** (*Ulex europaeus*), *aiteann* in Irish. A thorny, evergreen bush that blooms in March or April and flowers well into the fall and early winter. Its small yellow petals and green stems make golds. Bring gloves to harvest this plant, as its needles are sharp as cacti. It is said that Jesus's crown of thorns was made from this bush.

**Heather**, ling (*Calluna vulgaris*), and bell (*Erica cinerea*), *fraoch* in Irish. Bell blooms a month or so before ling in the summer. Heather gives a yellow dye and contains tannins for tanning leather. This plant dries well and can be used up to two years after it is cut for strong colours.

**Lady's bedstraw** (*Galium verum*), *ru Mhuire* or *baladh cnise* in Irish. A medium-tall wildflower with tiny bright yellow flowers, which bloom in early summer. It grows along hedges and in meadows, and its roots give a red dye.

In comparison to madder's pencil-thick roots, the bedstraw I loosened from the soil had hair-thin roots. I cannot imagine getting a red dye from this plant without collecting a ton of it, although Su Grierson reports that the plants living in sandy soil grow long roots with many side shoots. The bedstraw must be dried well, as this enables

*An Portach*, The Bog, Dermot Cannon, 29"x 42", natural dyes and handspun yarn.

Collection of Anne Ueltschi

Photo: Dermot Cannon

an enzyme in the roots to work best on the alizarin dye component of the plant.

In the old days in the Outer Hebrides one or two sacks of roots were sufficient for dyeing. The act was so common that in 1695 a Soil Preservation Act was passed that prohibited the pulling of the plant along the sea, which led to clandestine night raids. Historically, lady's bedstraw was also collected for its fragrance to stuff mattresses. According to Bríd Mahon, its Irish name, *baladh cnise,* is derived from the folk belief that it was one of the herbs in Christ's manger.

**Peat and bog ore,** *oubac* in Irish. Earth found in a bog. When simmered in a dyepot with purple loosestrife, it produced a silver-green on wool.

A footnote in *Ireland Industrial and Agricultural* states that bog-ore gives a dull black.[5] This validates what Jimmy Carr mentioned during our dye workshop about 'pig iron or iron ore'.

In his novel, *Bogmail,* author Patrick McGinley mentions *ruamheirg,* for which there is no English word. It means the red discolouration of mountain water from iron ore. In many cases, the very water of Glencolmcille acts as a mordant to sadden dye colours.[6]

**Purple loosestrife** (*Lythrum salicaria*). Bríd Mahon cites a purple dye from the flowers of this tall, purple flowering plant which blooms in summer and late fall. My experiments with these plants, picked from the roadside in July near Doolin, yielded a saturated brown using an iron mordant, but not as dark as that of knotted wrack.[7]

While this plant is known for its mystical qualities, my association with this cheerful wildflower, which towers above most in the landscape is, the image I captured in a photograph of a field full of loosestrife between Letterkenny and Ramelton. It was just after a storm, and the sky held black and yellow-grey clouds, and the sun shone behind all the mist. A shaft of light caused a vivid rainbow to rise up from the purple stalks of loosestrife.

The plant, which was used in the seventeenth century for eye lotions contains tannins, which help mineral pigments bond to wool. For this reason, Taipéis Gael has used purple loosestrife in the dyepot with turf to obtain a silvery sage.

**Ragwort** (*Senecio jacobaea*), *Buachallán buí* in Irish. A wildflower that grows in fields and along roadsides. Both the stem and flowers give a yellow dye.

Ragwort is best to harvest in August. I have made brighter yellows from this than the golds from gorse. A frozen gallon of a left-over dyebath gave a brassier yellow dye than a brew I had made from the fresh flowers a year earlier.

In *Colour Cauldron,* Su Grierson notes, 'Ragwort is more generally known as

*Stinking Willie,* a name that owes something to the unpleasant odour of the plant, to its invading nature and the Scots detestation of William, Duke of Cumberland, leader of the victorious crown troops at the Battle of Culloden'.[8] On the contrary, I find this plant quite sweet-smelling.

Ragwort contains six toxic substances. If consumed by livestock it can cause liver damage and its seeds can be poisonous to people. It is always best to dye in a well-ventilated area, or out of doors, wearing a painter's mask and gloves.

In the novel *Bogmail,* the weed becomes the bane of the policeman's existence when he is charged with the eradication of this plant by order of the Department of Agriculture and Fisheries. In this excerpt McGing says to Roarty:

'Every field I clap eyes on is yellow with it. Some farmers seem to grow nothing else. They know it's poison: you'd think they'd do something about it without waiting to be pestered by me'.

'It's the way of fallen flesh', said Roarty.

'It's a disgrace that a policeman of my experience should have nothing better to think about than ragwort'.[9]

**Tree lichens** (*Lobaria pulmonaria*), *crotal* in Irish. A silver-green rosette or fungus that grows on old trees, especially oak and maple, and yields an auburn or rusty brown dye on wool.

Professor Michael Mitchell at NUI Galway indicated that they were given their old English common name, lungwort, due to their lung-like appearance. According to Bolton, in *Lichens for Vegetable Dyeing,* a folk medicine made with this lichen was prepared into a jelly for those suffering from pulmonary infection. This plant is currently endangered in the British Isles.

**Weld** (*Receda luteola*), *buí mór* in Irish. A biennial plant forming a rosette of leaves in the first year and yellow flowers in the second. It yields a true yellow dye. 'The prettiest' of all yellows, according to William Morris.

Weld was often used as an under-dye with indigo or with woad for green. The yellow from weld is not only the prettiest, but it is also the most colour-fast to light – its colour lasting for centuries. This is to be contrasted to other yellow-yielding Irish dyeplants, such as ragwort, which may fade considerably within two weeks if placed in direct sunlight.

It is important that dyers keep the end use in mind when choosing the right dye materials. For instance, dyers might use a more fugitive dyestuff with everyday items, such as socks or knitted hats, which could easily be tossed back into the leftover liquid of any dyepot to revive its colour; however, a colour-fast dyestuff, such as weld, should be used for tartans and tapestries.

## Imported Traditional Dyestuffs

As reported in *Ireland Industrial and Agricultural,* the export of Irish wool to any country other than England was prohibited along with the import of dyestuffs into Ireland during the era around the reign of Charles I and II. Some of the more commonly used imported dyes are listed below.[10]

**Cochineal** (*Dactylopius coccus*). Dried bodies of a wingless female insect that feeds off cacti in Mexico. Its carbamic acid makeup makes a purplish-red or magenta dye. When used with a tin mordant, cochineal yields scarlet.

It was used by the Mexican and Aztec Indians for dyeing and was brought back to Spain in the sixteenth century. Colonies of the bugs were established on the Canary Islands. Given Ireland's history of trading with Spain, it is possible that the dyestuff would have been used in medieval Ireland, just as it was for tartans in Scotland.

**Indigo** (*Indigo tinctoria*), *pluirin* in Irish. A blue dye obtained from plant of the legume family, of which there are over 300 species known. Most are similar in form. Its foliage grows three to six feet tall with erect stems and few branches. Their leaves fold up at night and unfold in daylight. From midsummer to autumn, clusters of bronze flowers develop at the leaf axials and on the ends of the branches. Indigo thrives in hot, humid climates and grows in full sun. 100 lb of fresh indigo stalks yield 4 oz of dye pigment. However, this well-saturated dye goes a long way; 1 oz will dye pounds and pounds of wool.

Dyers in India and Southeast Asia have dyed with indigo for thousands of years. Its Arabic name, *anil,* led to 'aniline' dyes. The Greeks and Romans imported indigo calling it *indicum,* meaning 'from India', which led to the word indigo. The Romans used indigo for cosmetics, paint, medical purposes and dyeing cloth.[11]

The extraction of dye from indigo leaves is a complicated process. First, leaves are heated in water. Oxygen is introduced by stirring, which causes the indoxly that seeps out of the plants to turn blue. The blue sludge often settles on the bottom of the pot and can be removed, dried and stored.

From this stone, a dye is made by preparing a reducing agent or something that dissolves the non-water-soluble stone. Vats of urine, bran and madder have been used historically. Today, sulphuric acid is used. A household product that contains lye will suffice.

Many believed indigo stones were mined. Marco Polo dispelled this myth after his travels to Asia in the thirteenth century. Indigo, in stone form, allowed for ease of exportation, first via caravans along the Silk Road and later in trading vessels by sea – which made the dyestuff more accessible and affordable.

*Port*, Monica de Bath, 29"x48," commercial yarn, natural dyes. Monica made this piece just after she moved from Donegal to Kildare. Rooted in 12,000 years of history from the boglands, this tapestry was woven as part of a community-based project, *Guth on bPortach*, Voice from the Bog. This is an arts initiative in which the young and old develop a visual language in weaving, clay and paint in Rathangan, where Monica now lives. 'At a time when the bog is being cut away, ideas develop to regenerate what was once Peatlands. The people of this bogside village face the challenge of a community in transition'. Dyes for this work are made of peat and heathers that speak to environmental awareness.

Collection of Monica de Bath

Photo: Adrian Melia

Spanish explorers found indigo in Central and South America where it was used as a dye for fabric, paint for bodies, and tints for clay. Common knowledge held that 1 lb of indigo was worth 10 lb of woad. It is no wonder indigo replaced domestic woad in Europe by the 1700s.

**Madder** (*Rubia tinctoria, Rubia peregrina* and *Sherardia arvensis*), *Madar or dearg faille* in Irish. The roots, which are woody and large in comparison to the plant itself, give a red dye. A minimum of three years of root growth is required before harvesting from a home garden but the longer one waits the better.

There is no more fitting introduction for this wildflower, which grows in Ireland, than Tim Robinson's account in *Stones of Aran: Labyrinth*. 'I will never see flowers that like again', he states,

> each one suddenly shining not only out of the wet rock or decayed undergrowth around it but out of the time in which that space had been dark, as if a beam had arrived at last, rejoicing, from a star formed long ago, light years away. It was not the famous rarities or even the one or two new discoveries I made that most enthralled me, but the underfoot beneath-notice nearly-nothings; the field madder, for instance, its mauve four-petalled blossoms … in clusters of a dozen … [12]

Madder has been widely cultivated in Europe and the Far East, and, according to Lillias Mitchell, it has also been cultivated in south-west Britain, the Burren and the Aran Islands. The latter two places grow field madder (*Sherardia arvensis*).[13] The red sails of hookers and the women's red skirts, once common to the Aran Islands, were dyed with madder.

In Turkey, madder is often used in carpets. It grows in the wild and in large plots, and is harvested after seven years with a tractor. A pulverizing machine is brought to the field for crunching the roots on location. Village dye masters use madder by the wheelbarrow full. I would propose that it is likely that madder seeds arrived in the Aran Islands via boats from the Mediterranean fertile crescent. An idea that sprouted after reading Bob Quinn's book *The Atlantean Irish* about the connections between Ireland and the East.

**Saffron** (*Crocus sativus*), *croch na mbanta* in Irish. Extracted from the yellow-orange stigma of the crocus flower more commonly known in Greece and the Middle East, it yields a rich, yellow dye.

Used in ancient times by Phoenicians and others, saffron was grown in Spain by the tenth century and imported to Ireland in the sixteenth. This was about the same time indigo became available.

Bríd Mahon points out that this dye was costly and therefore fell into disuse in Ireland, where so many other native plants would give a yellow dye.

'The Irish and Scots wore "saffron" shirts', Su Grierson said, noting that it was more likely not actual saffron, but the less expensive weld or native plants such as bog myrtle, or *roid*.[14] I would agree with Grierson, as my experience with Mexican and Persian saffron has been that it is quite fugitive, fading drastically in direct sunlight. Weld is far more fast to light and washing.

**Woad** (*Isatis tinctoria*), *glaisin* in Irish. A tall biennial plant that forms a rosette of leaves, which are the source of its blue dye.

In order to use this plant, which is grouped with other indigotin sources such as indigo and whelks, a similar fermentation process to indigo is required. Per plant, woad produces less indigotin than indigo, so once the indigo trade began to flourish, woad became the less-preferred dye plant. Apparently, the indigo trade's effect on woad-producing European towns was economically devastating.

Documentation has shown the use of woad in early Britian, with the Romans reporting the use of it there as a body paint; fragments of woad stems have also turned up in Viking excavations in York. As further evidence, several of the ninth- to eleventh-century British textiles reveal indigotin, probably from woad, since indigo – a non-native plant – would not have been available for another four centuries.

The Celts are also believed to have used woad, colouring their skin with its juice, but probably not only as a means to make themselves more fierce-looking in battle, as some have suggested, because we know that the women and children used it too. Evidently, the juice could be extracted without a fermentation process suggesting the dye was topical and may have washed off readily.

During the Middle Ages woad became the dominant dyestuff in northern Europe. The leaves had a medicinal use for healing wounds and ulcers. It was probably brought to Ireland from Scotland early on, as it has no known natural native occurrence.


## Mordants

Mordants are mineral compounds such as alum, iron, and copper that help wool absorb dyes, giving brighter, deeper and more saturated colours. They help create a bond between the cellulose molecules of plants and the protein molecules of sheep fibres. They also increase the dye's fastness or permanence to light and washing.

Different mordants will affect the end colour of a dye. For example, iron tends to sadden colours, turning a yellow a more brown-gold. Copper tends to darken colours and give them a green cast. Tin brightens. Copper, iron or aluminum pots can also act as mordants.

During Taipéis Gael's dye workshop, we used alum except when dyeing with indigo, whelks and lichens, none of which require a mordant.

# Afterword:
# A Future for Taipéis Gael?

The year 2005 marked Taipéis Gael's tenth anniversary. It is only fitting to recall with pride some of their achievements: exhibitions on three continents; hundreds of tapestries to their credit; playing host to an international community of artists; and the growth of these individuals from students to teachers within their own communities and abroad. They've reshaped and retold the skills and stories taught to them by their own mentors, and their work hangs in halls and homes from Perth to Pisa. The fruit of their labour has been documented in magazines, journals of Irish and women's studies, television programmes, websites, a PhD dissertation, and now this book.

Who and what is to be credited for all of this? The determination, courage and creativity of each of the artists; their mentors and the administrator; their community that gave them encouragement; the development agencies (in particular Údarás na Gaeltachta and the local organization Oideas Gael) that had the good sense to recognize a worthwhile project when they saw one; the Arts Council and Aer Lingus, which flies these Irish artists and others abroad for exhibitions, compliments of the airline. A government that values art is also to be thanked, one – according to my understanding – that offers artists incentives to live in Ireland by way of tax-breaks. Lastly, the patrons of Taipéis Gael also deserve a great deal of recognition for their tremendous role in sustaining the cooperative for the last decade. All of these people and organizations have come together to help these weavers evolve into the confident and capable artists they are today.

Yet, for every headland or upland, there is a valley. In the spring of 2005 Taipéis Gael came to the decision to give up their studio and let their administrator go because they simply hadn't the funds to retain either. While the weavers look to the future in anticipation of continuing their collaborative relationship, they will now weave from their own homes in the fashion of most solo artists. Dermot Cannon, like the rest of the weavers who thrived within the group, will continue to be involved with wool, though now as the manager of his family flock rather than as a weaver at the loom. Máire McGinley has begun work on an Irish dictionary for the Royal Irish Academy. Margaret Cunningham is the new manager of the Glencolmcille Folk Museum and she has just finished a tapestry commission for St Killian's Gaelic College in County Monaghan. Annie McGinley has enrolled at the National University of Ireland, Galway, to study history and literature. Despite their individual endeavors, Taipéis Gael will continue to hold joint and solo exhibitions, and will also collaborate with other artists, accept commissions, teach workshops and maintain their name and website. They are morphing, so to speak, into a virtual cooperative.

What is responsible for such a shift? Annie McGinley cites diverse reasons such as the learning curve in pulling together such an organization; the constant struggle of pricing art; and funding that provides money primarily for capital expenditure. In their case, little equipment was needed other than wool, a computer and a printer. But strict grant and loan stipulations often ruled out adequate funding for administrative purposes – the very thing that would have benefited Taipéis Gael the most.

A wide-angle perspective might point to the consequences of 9/11, which caused tourism in Ireland to drop and not pick up for nearly two years. Simultaneously, much of the European Union funding that once seeded projects in Ireland like Taipéis Gael was diverted to new member states in Eastern Europe. Irish development agencies continue to court foreign investors whose interests may often be short term.

It is this author's opinion that foreign corporate investments are potentially the most detrimental to indigenous grass-roots enterprises. While boosting the economy according to the corporate model seems promising, often what is at stake is the cultural and economic sustainability of vibrant communities. Without selective and appropriate development policies, it seems to me that Ireland could become further enmeshed in the current trend towards a global economy, which breeds monoculture with the risk that connections to place and tradition are lost.

Taipéis Gael offers an alternative to these prevailing capital and energy-intensive business models. It uses few resources and as Annie McGinley mentioned, its products are 100 per cent natural. They could not be more in tune with place, tradition, and the planet. I believe it is here that a future lies for Taipéis Gael. They have already shown – through their stunning interplay of colour, shape and form – that qualitative endeavours are equally as important as the quantitative, that progress can be measured in terms of the inherent aesthetic value of place, of a sound environment and of connected communities. Their actions suggest that the world's clock might do well to calibrate itself to the pace of a weaver's shuttle – to find time to reflect on our current obsession with the bottom line and also to summon the foresight with which to consider the consequences of such perspectives. This could greatly benefit our exquisite endangered existence, not only in Ireland but also in our shared universe.

I pray that the powers that be will come to hold up Taipéis Gael as a shining example and help them generate more tapestries and more exhibitions. Thus they will help the next generation of artists from Glencolmcille to tell their stories, so that the people of Donegal will continue weaving their future.

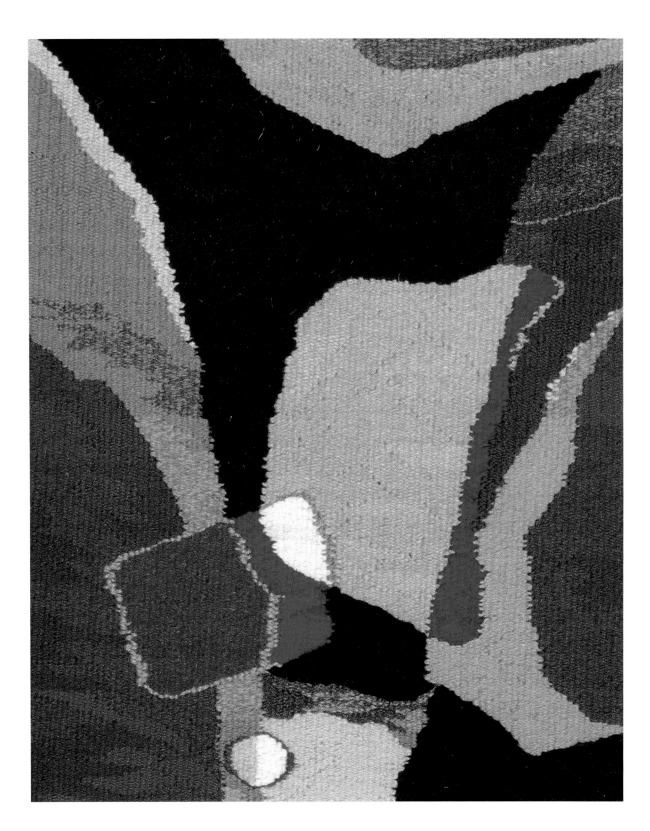

# Acknowledgements

Many people inspired the writing of this book. I hope that I have not forgotten anyone here; if so, you have my sincerest apologies in advance. Taipéis Gael and I also hope that we have credited the right people with respect to tapestry ownership and photo credits. Please inform the publisher with any concerns and corrections will be made in subsequent printings.

My deep appreciation to my comrade and photographer Laurence Boland, Dublin, for taking on this endeavor and remaining true to it for several years with no guarantee that it would lead anywhere.

In Glencolmcille and surrounding townlands I'd like to thank: Liam Ó Cuinneagáin, Oideas Gael; Monica de Bath, who divides her time between Glen and Kildare, for initially helping me understand the story of Taipéis Gael, and Taipéis Gael weavers and their mentors, whose stories grace these pages, for the years they patiently answered questions with respect to this manuscript and for allowing Laurence Boland to photograph them in their homes or at work for the benefit of this project. They include: Annie McGinley, Margaret Cunningham, Máire McGinley, Dermot Cannon, Conal McIntrye, Conal Gillespie, Sandra Mockler, Angela Bryne, Rose Hegarty, Mary McNelis, Mary Kate O'Gara, Con O'Gara and Jimmy Carr. Special thanks goes to Annie McGinley for taking the time to scan all of the tapestry slides for this book, and for answering my many emails to sort out details with respect

to this project. My gratitude extends also to the community of Glen for their welcoming hospitality, particularly Geraldine Byrne, who opened her bed-and-breakfast during the off season for me more than once. To Anthony Boyle and Seán O'Donnell, for discussing the ways of sheep with me on the roadside and at the Carrick Sheep market. Thanks also to Conal McGinley and his neighbours in Malinbeg for inviting Laurence Boland on a sheep-shearing expedition to Rathlin O'Beirne Island, which provided for a rare photo essay that is featured in this book.

The following people and institutions generously shared their knowledge and talents with me on various aspects of Irish arts and literature relative to weaving in Ireland: Brendan Larrissy, County Clare, and Eamonn O'Broithe, Galway, and Ríonach Uí Ógáin, Department of Irish Folklore, UCD, for help with traditional weaving and working songs; Galway Irish Language School for help with Irish words and phrases; Sally Skilling, Ulster Folk and Transport Museum, for songs and poems on weaving; Jackie Gamble, Emerald Books, Belfast, for digging up the few books on the old linen trade; Patricia O'Hanlon, librarian, National University Ireland at Galway, for surveys of weaving books and journals; Martin McNaulty, Marine Science Center NUI Galway, for information on dog whelks; Laura Kelly, Irish Seaweed Institute, for information on seaweeds that I used for dyes; the National

Left: *Journey to Forever*, Conal McIntyre, 20" x 30", Carpet yarn

Private collection

Photo: Conal McIntyre

Museum Ireland, for the opportunity to view spindle artefacts and whose photograph of such appears in this book; archaeologist Maria FitzGerald, PhD, Dublin, for information about the history of spinning and weaving in Ireland, and ancient textiles and spindles; Galway stone carver Denis Groggin for a replica of an ancient sandstone whorl; Galway woodworker Ollie Burke for a replica of an ancient yew spindle; Theresa O'Donohue, Doolin, for giving me a fleece of her rare breed Galway Sheep; Rosemary McCarron Corbitt, tapestry artist, Glenties, for sending me a sample of bog bean for my dye experiments; Mary Shiels, past president of the Guild of Irish Spinners, Dyers and Weavers, for participating in a dye workshop at Taipéis Gael; Larry Brownen, botanist, for her help in plant identification of Irish natural dyeplants; Mary O'Rourke, textile artist and designer, Dublin, for sending me Soay wool and answering numerous other questions with regard to spinning, dyeing and weaving; the Galway Claddagh Knitters, for their enthusiasm and knowledge about the Aran and Irish knitting practices and patterns; Dr Eileen Moore Quinn, College of Charleston, NC, for sharing with me her PhD dissertation, which included chapters on Taipéis Gael.

Many others have made suggestions on this manuscript, travelled with me to Glencolmcille for research, or gave me encouragement while writing this book: Marie and Carl Nordgren, Durham, NC, who also assisted me on wet and chilly days in Galway, Connemara, and Glencolmcille to collect lichen and whelk specimens for my natural dye experiments; Molly Danforth, for travelling with me twice to Glencolmcille; Lora Hughes who also provided good company on the road to Taipéis Gael and offered suggestions on this manuscript. I'd like to thank Galway writers, poets and playwrights: Máire Holmes; the late Billy Pope and the Galway Retired Writers Group, who provided a sounding board for early drafts of the text; Kevin Whelan, for answering my numerous questions on 'things Irish', and cheering me on. My friends Seán and Bridget Hawkins, for feeding me home-cooked meals; likewise many thanks to my cousin, Anne Higgins and her husband Tim, for treating me to dinners in Galway; Freda and Owen Cunningham, for offering me a bed on many, many occasions; Theresa and Martin Nolan, for bottomless cups of tea and conversation; Patricia and Mike O'Hanlon, for their encouragement and for minding my children from time to time while I dashed about in pursuit of yet another thread of Irish weaving lore.

Several of my weaver friends in the United States helped with technical aspects of the craft for my earlier articles about Taipéis Gael: Anne Adams, Moscow, Idaho, who participated in a dye workshop in Glencolmcille; the Palouse Empire Weavers and Spinners Guild; Jaynee Koch, a wellspring of knowledge and a patient teacher; Hog Heaven Spinners, Moscow, Idaho; Sarah Swett, tapestry artist, Moscow, Idaho, who read sections of this book and sent me dye stuffs and skeins of yarn for my research, in times of need.

I owe much gratitude to my Spokane writing group for critiquing this manuscript: Mary Douthitt, Claire Rudolph Murphy, Mary Cronk Farrell, Lynn Caruso, Marie Whalen and Patricia Nikolina Clark. Thanks also to Mariah Kalstad for last minute typing and errands. Special thanks goes to Lisa Frank, a writer and editor who pushed up her sleeves in the eleventh hour to help me. Her skills and focus helped shape this manuscript into a cohesive whole. It then went out into the world to be chosen by the Irish Heritage Council as one of the books to be funded in 2006. Thus, my hearty thanks goes to the Heritage Council. Thanks also to Tom Dunne, Mike Collins, Sophie Watson, Caroline Somers and Lucy Freeman at Cork University Press for publishing this collection in such a timely and professional manner. Thanks also to Sara Wilbourne, formerly of the Press, for her initial acquisition of this book. I would like to recognize Pádraig O'Aholáin and Údarás na Gaeltachta for their early contribution toward my research, and my dear friend Laurie MacMillan, who designed my website and has donated countless hours of web work to this project.

With fondness I think about my friends whom I did not mention in my prologue, but who traveled with my sister Eileen Clapp and me so many years ago to Glencolmcille and explored the souterrain with us: Katie Reish Gardner, Marianne Koehler Sullivan and Patty Donohue.

Finally, my heartfelt thanks always to my husband, Bill, and my children, Conor, Maeve and Gaelen for their good nature in the face of my ruminations and ramblings abroad while working on this book. My appreciation extends also to my siblings and relatives for their encouragement, and to my parents for their help with research, needed phrases, and for passing on their happy obsession with Ireland to me. Much gratitude to all the sheep – on both sides of the Atlantic – who donated their wool for the cause.

PERMISSIONS

I would like to thank the following editors and publishers for their previously published essays and articles related to this book: Jim Rogers, *New Hibernia Review,* for the prologue and two essays about mentors Mary McNelis and Con O'Gara in 'Conversations in Donegal' (Autumn 2001); Letitia Pollard, *Ireland of the Welcomes* magazine, for 'Ancestral Landscape' (Dec. 1996); Marilyn Murphy and Amy Clark Moore, Interweave Press, for 'James Shiels: The Last Master Spinning Wheelwright of Ireland', *Spin Off* (Winter 2000) and 'Irish Tapestry Weavers Find a Bit of Home in the American Southwest', *Spin Off* (Fall 1997); and Sandra Bowles, Handweavers Guild of America, 'Taipéis Gael: An Ancestral Landscape', *Shuttle, Spindle and Dyepot* (Fall 1996).

Many thanks to the following people and establishments and to others whom I may have failed to mention, who have photographed their tapestry collections for the benefit of this book: President Mary Mac Aleese; Joseph M. Murphy, Country Bank, Scarsdale, New York, and Jo Vicker, Photo Bureau; Alice and Charles Beamer and Mark Butler; Samuel Couch; Ann Ueltschi; Father McKee, St. Joseph's Church, Beltsville, Maryland; Adrian Melia; Horizons; The National Concert Hall, Dublin; The Glen Hotel, Malin Mor; Dr. Eileen Moore Quinn; Liam O'Cúinneagáin, Oideas Gael; Michael O'Doherty; Letterkenny Regional Technical College; ChromoStat Photography, Spokane, Washington; Letterkenny Arts Centre; Susan Gallagher and William Durham; Michael Herity; Údarás Na Gaeltachta; Conal McIntyre; Lar Boland and Taipéis Gael.

*Waterfall*, 20"x 36",
Margaret Cunningham.
This waterfall is
just northwest of
Port, a village near
Glencolmcille.

# References

## Introduction

1 Eileen Moore Quinn. '*Nostalgia is Our Future: Self-Representational Genres and Cultural Revival in Ireland*'. (UMI Dissertation Services, 1999), p.64.

2 Kinnfaela (McGinley, T.C.), *The Cliff Scenery of South-Western Donegal* (Dublin: Fourmasters Press Ltd, 2000).

3 Patrick McGinley, *Bogmail* (New York: Ticknor & Fields, 1981).

4 David Shaw Smith, *Ireland's Traditional Crafts* (New York: Thames & Hudson, 1984).

5 Fergus Kelly, *A Guide to Early Irish Law* (Dublin: Dublin Institute for Advanced Studies, 1988).

6 Judith Hoad, *This is Donegal Tweed* (Donegal: Shoestring Publications, 1987).

7 William P. Coyne (ed.), *Ireland: Industrial and Agricultural* (Dublin, Browne and Nolan, 1902), p. 218.

8 Ibid., p. 440.

## Mentors

1 Judith Hoad, *This is Donegal Tweed* (Donegal: Shoestring Publications, 1987).

2 Henry Glassie, *The Spirit of Folk Art: The Girard Collection at the Museum of International Folk Art* (New York: Henry N. Abrams Inc., 1989).

## Tools

1 Nelson and Walsh, *Trees of Ireland* (Dublin: Lilliput Press, 1993), p.221

2 John Matthews, *The Druid Source Book* (London: Blanford 1997), pp. 76, 77, 83.

3 Elizabeth Wayland Barber, *Women's Work: The First 20,000 Years* (New York: W.W. Norton & Company, New York, 1994), pp. 235–8.

4 John Mathews, *The Druid Source Book,* p. 83.

5 Ibid, p. 37

6 David Shaw Smith, *Ireland's Traditional Crafts,* p. 19.

7 Ibid, p. 19.

## Raw Materials

1 National Public Radio Programmes, 'Sheep Smarts' (US: November, 2001).

2 Deborah Robson (ed.), *Handspun Treasures for Rare Wools: Collected Works from Save the Sheep Project* (Loveland: Interweave Press, 2000), pp. 6, 9.

3 Anne-Marie Moroney, 'Galway Sheep', *Spin Off* (Fall 1990), pp. 36–9.

## Natural Dyes

1 Fergus Kelly, *A Guide to Early Irish Law* (Dublin: Dublin Institute for Advanced Studies, 1988),

2 Laurence Ginnell, *The Brehon Laws* (London: T. Fisher, 1894).

3 Belfast Natural History and Philosophy Society (information on madder root seeds at an archaeological site in Fermanagh).

4 Emily V. Murray, School of Geosciences, The Queen's University of Belfast, from email letter regarding her doctoral thesis on the procurement of purple shellfish dyes in Ireland.

5 P.W. Joyce, *A Social History of Ancient Ireland* (vol. 2), p. 357. (Irish Genealogical Society 1997)

6 Su Grierson, *The Colour Cauldron* (Perth: Mill Books, 1986), p. 66.

7 Emily V. Murray.

8 Brid Mahon, 'Traditional Dyestuffs in Ireland' in Alan Gailey and Daithi Ó hÓgáin (eds.), *Gold Under the Furze: Studies in Folk Tradition* (Dublin: Glendale Press), pp. 22, 122.

## A Glossary of Dyes

1 E. Estyn Evans, *Irish Folk Ways* (London, Routledge & Kegan Paul, 1957).

2 Becker, Heinrich. *Seaweed Memories* (Dublin: Wolfhound Press, 2001)

3 Michael D. Guiry, 'Research and Development of a Sustainable Irish Seaweed Industry'. *Occasional Papers in Irish Science and Technology* (1997).

4 Eileen M. Bolton, *Lichens for Vegetable Dyeing* (McMinnville: Robin & Russ Handweavers, 1991), p. 9.

5 William P. Coyne (ed.), *Ireland: Industrial and Agricultural* (Dublin: Browne & Nolan, 1902)

6 Patrick McGinley, *Bogmail.* (New York: Ticknor & Fields. 1981)

7 Brid Mahon, 'Traditional Dyestuffs in Ireland'.

8 Su Grierson, *The Colour Cauldron,* pp. 169, 172, 191, 201, 205–7 and 217.

9 Patrick McGinley, *Bogmail,* p. 70

10 William P. Coyne, *Ireland Industrial and Agricultural.*

11 Rita Buchanan, A *Weaver's Garden* (Loveland: Interweave Press, 1987), p. 105.

12 Tim Robinson, *Stones of Aran: Labyrinth* (Dublin: Lilliput Press, 1995), p. 305

13 Lilias Mitchell, *Irish Weaving: Discoveries and Personal Experiences* (Dundalk: Dundalgan Press Ltd, 1986).

14 Su Grierson, *The Colour Cauldron* (Perth: Mill Books, 1986)

# Further Reading

Barber, Elizabeth Wayland. *Women's Work: The First 20,000 Years* (New York: W.W. Norton & Company, 1994).

Becker, Heinrich. *Seaweed Memories.*(Dublin: Wolfhound Press, 2001).

Bolton, Eileen M. *Lichens for Vegetable Dyeing* (McMinnville: Robin & Russ Handweavers, 1991).

Buchanan, Rita. *A Weaver's Garden* (Loveland: Interweave Press, 1987).

Buick, Rev. George Raphael. "The Weaver Question". *Poems From College and Country by Three Brothers* (Belfast: W&G Baird, 1900).

Clark, Wallace. *Linen on the Green* (Belfast: The University Press, 1982).

Coyne, William P. (ed.) *Ireland: Industrial and Agricultural* (Dublin: Browne and Nolan, 1902).

De Waal, Esther. *The Celtic Way of Prayer* (New York: Doubleday, 1997).

Evans, E. Estyn. *Irish Folk Ways* (London: Routledge & Kegan Paul, 1957).

—. *Irish Heritage: The Landscape, the People and Their Work* (Dundalk: Dundalgan Press, 1942).

Gifford, Jane. *The Wisdom of Trees: Mysteries, Magic, and Medicine* (New York: Godsfield Press, 2000).

Ginnell, Laurence. *The Brehon Laws* (London: T. Fisher, 1894).

Glassie, Henry. *All Silver and No Brass: An Irish Christmas Mumming* (Dingle: Brandon Book Publishers, 1983).

—. *The Spirit of Folk Art: The Girard Collection at the Museum of International Folk Art* (New York: Henry N. Abrams, 1989).

*Gleann Cholm Cille: Seoid oidhreacht na hÉireann: Rich in Ireland's Heritage* (GlenColmcille: Oideas Gael, 1997).

Graves, Alfred Perceval. "Spinning Wheel Song". *The Irish Poems of Alfred Perceval Graves:Countryside Songs, Songs and Ballads* (Dublin: Maunsel & Company, 1908).

Grierson, Su. *The Colour Cauldron* (Perth: Mill Books, 1986).

Herity, Michael. *Gleanncholmcille: A Guide to 5,000 Years of History in Stone* (Baile Atha Cliath: Na Clocha Breaca, 1993).

Hiscock, Sue, *A Field Key to the British Brown Seaweeds (Phaeophyta)* (Galway: Marine Sciences Institute, UCG, 1979).

Hoad, Judith. *This is Donegal Tweed* (Donegal: Shoestring Publications Inver, 1987).

Howson, Christine M. and Bernard E. Picton (eds.). *The Species Directory of the Marine Fauna and Flora of the British Isles and Surrounding Seas* (Belfast: Marine Conservatory Society).

Kelly, Fergus. *A Guide to Early Irish Law* (Dublin: Dublin Institute for Advanced Studies, 1988).

Kinnfaela (McGinley, T.C.). *The Cliff Scenery of South-Western Donegal* (Dublin: Fourmasters Press, 2000).

Lisburn, Thomas Campbell. 'The Spinner Girl's Song'. *Lays from Lisnagarvey* (Belfast: John Reid & Co., 1884).

Matthews, John. *The Druid Source Book* (London: Blanford, 1997).

McClintock, H.F. *Old Irish and Highland Dress* (1943).

M'Comb, William. 'The Spinning Wheel'. *The Poetical Works of William M'Comb* (Belfast: Hamliton, Adams and Co).

McGinley, Patrick. *Bogmail* (New York: Ticknor & Fields, 1981).

Mitchell, H. Lillias. *Irish Weaving: Discoveries and Personal Experiences* (Dundalk: Dundalgan Press, 1986).

Nelson and Walsh. *Trees of Ireland.* (Dublin: Lilliput Press, 1993).

*New Departures: A Review of Developments in Horizon-(Disadvantaged)* (Dublin: WRC Social and Economic Consultation Ltd., 1994).

Gailey, Alan and Ó hÓgáin, Daithi. *Gold Under the Furze: Studies in Folk Tradition* (Dublin: Glendale Press.

Quinn, Bob. *The Atlantean Irish* (Dublin: Lilliput Press, 2005).

Quinn, Eileen Moore. 'Nostalgia is Our Future: Self-Representational Genres and Cultural Revival in Ireland'. (UMI Dissertation Services, 1999).

Robinson, Tim. *Stones of Aran: Labyrinth* (Dublin: Lilliput Press, 1995).

Robson, Deborah (ed.) *Handspun Treasures for Rare Wools: Collected Works from Save the Sheep Project* (Loveland: Interweave Press, 2000).

Ryder, M.L. *Sheep: Man* (London: Gerald Duckworth, 1983).

Scallan, Christine. *Irish Herbal Cures.*

Shane, Elizabeth. 'The Hill Woman'. *Tales of the Donegal Coast and Islands* (London: Selwyn & Blount, 1921).

Sharkey, Olive. *Old Days, Old Ways* (Dublin: The O'Brien Press, 1985).

*Ways of Old: Traditional Life in Ireland* (Dublin: The O'Brien Press, 1985).

Smith, David Shaw. *Ireland's Traditional Crafts* (London: Thames & Hudson, 1984).

Stokes, Whitley. 'Lines of Saints'. *Book of Lismore* (New York: Ams Press, 1989).

Waller, John Francis. 'The Spinning-Wheel' in Stopford A. Brooke and T.W. Rolleston (eds), *A Treasury of Irish Poetry in the English Tongue* (London: Smith, Elder & Co., 1900).

## Related Magazine Articles

'An Ancient Tool Rediscovered'. *Spin Off.* Spring 1995: 50–51.

Bateman, Wendy E. 'Back to Basics–Woolen Spinning'. *Shuttle Spindle & Dyepot.* Winter 2000/2001: 37–40.

Buchanan, Rita. 'A Closer Look: Woolen/Worsted, R.I.P'. *Spin Off.* Spring 2001: 34–37.

Clarke, Amy C. 'Save the Sheep'. *Spin Off.* Spring 2000: 40–43.

Erikson, Deb. 'Merging an Ancient Art with a Modern Tool'. *Spin Off.* Spring 2001: 74–79.

Irwin, Bobbie. 'An Ode to Woad'. *Spin Off.* Summer 1997: 86–92.

—. 'Colors from the North Country: Research in Large-Scale'. *Spin Off.* Spring 2000: 87–89.

Miller, Dorothy. 'Putting Indigo to Sleep'. *Spin Off.* Spring 2000: 77–79.

Moroney, Anne-Marie. 'Galway Sheep'. *Spin Off.* Fall 1990: 36–39.

Rhodes, Carol Huebscer. 'Wool Classing School'. *Spin Off.* Fall 2000: 34–37.

Robson, Deborah. 'Rare Wools from Rare Sheep, Part 2'. *Spin Off.* Spring 1999: 90–93.

Skinner, Nancy. 'Saxon Green'. *Spin Off.* Summer 1997: 83–85.

Szostak, Rosemarie. 'Soay: Stone-Age Fiber'. *Spin Off.* Summer 1995: 62–65.

## Internet Articles

'Cheviot'.
www.ansi.okstate.edu/breeds/SHEEP/CHEVIOT/

'Learning About Linen'.
www.thelinenhouse.com

'Scottish Blackface'.
www.ansi.okstate.edu/breeds/sheep/SCOTTISH/index.html

'Sheep Smarts'.
www.npr.org/programs/atc/features/2001/nov/sheep/011107.sheep.html